# Land an

# Land and Sea
## A World-Historical Meditation

Carl Schmitt

Translated by Samuel Garrett Zeitlin

Edited and with Introductions by
Russell A. Berman and Samuel Garrett Zeitlin

Telos Press Publishing
Candor, NY

Copyright © 2015 Telos Press Publishing

All rights reserved. No portion of this book may be reproduced or transmitted in any form by any means, electronic, mechanical, photocopying, recording, or otherwise, without permission in writing from the publisher. For information on getting permission for reprints or excerpts, contact telos@telospress.com.

Printed in the United States of America
19   18   17   16   15      1   2   3   4

Translated by permission from the German original, *Land und Meer: Eine weltgeschichtliche Betrachtung*, © 1942, 1981 Klett-Cotta—J. G. Cotta'sche Buchhandlung Nachfolger GmbH, Stuttgart.

Translation copyright © 2015 Samuel Garrett Zeitlin

The first edition of this book appeared in 1942 in Leipzig, the second edition appeared in 1954 in Stuttgart, the third edition in 1981 in Cologne, the fourth in 1993, the fifth in 2001, and the sixth edition in 2007 as well appeared with Klett-Cotta in Stuttgart. The present translation follows the seventh edition from 2011, which itself follows the third edition from 1981.

ISBN: 978-0-914386-56-8

Library of Congress Cataloging-in-Publication Data

Schmitt, Carl, 1888-1985.
  [Land und Meer. English]
  Land and sea : a world-historical meditation / Carl Schmitt ; translated by Samuel Garrett Zeitlin ; edited and with introductions by Russell A. Berman and Samuel Garrett Zeitlin.
     pages cm
  Includes bibliographical references.
  ISBN 978-0-914386-56-8 (pbk.)
  1. Geopolitics. 2. Sea-power. I. Berman, Russell A., 1950- editor of compilation. II. Zeitlin, Samuel Garrett, editor of compilation. III. Title.
  JC319.S3913 2015
  320.1'2—dc23
                              2015027043

Cover design by Amanda Trager and Erik Moskowitz

Telos Press Publishing
PO Box 811
Candor, NY 13743

www.telospress.com

# Contents

Note on the Edition and Translation
vii

Acknowledgments
xi

Geography, Warfare, and the Critique of Liberalism
in Carl Schmitt's *Land and Sea*
*Russell A. Berman*
xiii

Propaganda and Critique:
An Introduction to *Land and Sea*
*Samuel Garrett Zeitlin*
xxxi

Land and Sea:
A World-Historical Meditation
*Carl Schmitt*
1

Works Consulted
99

## Note on the Edition and Translation

In a letter to Carl Schmitt dated October 20, 1938, following a reading of Schmitt's book *Der Leviathan*, Ernst Jünger wrote, "I have the feeling that, when the opportunity arises, you must write a work without the apparatus of references, to some extent with a second *naïveté*, which you would wear well."[1] The 1942 edition of *Land und Meer* was almost entirely "a work without the apparatus of references"—bearing only a single footnote while nonetheless containing numerous quotations, many of which were of unspecified provenance. The 1954 and 1981 editions of *Land und Meer* expanded the number of footnotes to two, while maintaining many quotations that were either unmarked or opaque or without an explicit source.

The present edition of *Land and Sea* is not "without the apparatus of references." While the original footnotes have been marked as such, other notes have been added in part to provide some clarification of references potentially obscure and in part with the aim of historical accuracy in conveying the variants between the various editions that Schmitt published during his lifetime.

The present translation of Carl Schmitt's *Land und Meer: Eine weltgeschichtliche Betrachtung* translates the seventh edition of the work published by Klett-Cotta in Stuttgart in 2011. This edition is a reprint of the third edition published in Cologne by Hohenheim in 1981. With the exception of an added afterword and a new pagination, some minor omissions,

---

1. Ernst Jünger–Carl Schmitt, *Briefe 1930–1983*, ed. Helmuth Kiesel, 2nd ed. (Stuttgart: Klett-Cotta, 2012 [1999]), p. 78.

and several typographic alterations, the third edition is based upon the text of the second edition published by Reclam in Stuttgart in 1954. The postwar second edition of *Land und Meer* contains substantial alterations to the first edition of Schmitt's work published by Reclam in Leipzig in 1942. The differences between the 1954 and 1942 editions, particularly in sections 3, 16, 17, 19, and 20, relate principally (though not exclusively) to Schmitt's depiction and characterization of the English and the Jewish people, and these textual alterations have been noted in footnotes to the present translation. In translating *Land and Sea*, the 1981, 1954, and 1942 editions of the text were compared with one another, along with the 1952 Spanish translation by Rafael Fernandez-Quintanilla, *Tierra y Mar: Consideraciones sobre la historia universal* (Madrid: Instituto de Estudios Políticos [Colección Civitas], 1952), which retains many of the passages omitted in the 1954 German edition. In addition, the notes and references have benefitted from an examination of Giovanni Gurisatti's apparatus to his 2002 Italian translation, *Terra e mare: Una riflessione sulla storia del mondo* (Milan: Adelphi Edizioni, 2011 [2002]), as well as Franco Volpi's expository essay in that volume, "Il potere degli elementi," which contains a list of variants between the 1942 and 1954 editions of Schmitt's German text (ibid., pp. 146–47), which have been followed as well as expanded upon in the notes to the current translation and edition.

This edition aims to provide an accurate translation of Schmitt's German within the limits of readable English, while preserving something of the tenor and tone of the Schmitt's original text. To this end, contractions were occasionally deployed in the English to maintain something of the informality, sharpness, and speed of *Land and Sea*. However, technical terms in Schmitt's political vocabulary, such as constitution (*Verfassung*), element (*Element*), power (*Macht*), and space (*Raum*), have been rendered consistently throughout the translation to allow English readers to track and interpret Schmitt's concepts, terminology, and usage.

Two such terms that merit sensitive treatment are *Völkerrecht* and *der Mensch*, both of which are deployed by Schmitt with some frequency throughout *Land and Sea*. It is not clear, for a variety of reasons, that Schmitt understands his notion of "the human" (*der Mensch*) to cover all that a contemporary reader might understand to be pertinent to the species *homo sapiens*. For reasons of philological and historical accuracy, in order to allow English readers to interpret Schmitt's notion of "the human" and to make both his political vocabulary as well as his political anthropology accessible to an English readership, *der Mensch* and its equivalents have been rendered as "the human" or "human" throughout. Similarly, it is not clear from the context and from Schmitt's other writings in the period 1937–43 that Schmitt understands by *Völkerrecht* everything that a contemporary reader might understand by "international law," with Schmitt identifying *Völkerrecht* with the *ius gentium* tradition of Roman law and claiming that certain states and peoples may not be subjects of *Völkerrecht*,[2] whatever "international law" or "so-called international law [*das sogenannte internationales Recht*]" may say to the contrary. In articles from 1940, in the period in which Schmitt claimed he began to write *Land and Sea*, Schmitt explicitly contrasted his notion of *Völkerrecht* with prevailing notions of "international law," offering the latter term in quotation marks in English in his German-language texts.[3] For these reasons, *Völkerrecht* has

---

2. Cf. Carl Schmitt, *Völkerrechtliche Großraumordnung* (Dritte, unveränderte Auflage der Ausgabe von 1941) (Berlin: Duncker & Humblot, 2007 [1941]), pp. 11, 59.
3. Cf. Carl Schmitt, "Die Auflösung der europäischen Ordnung im 'International Law' (1890–1939)," in *Deutsche Rechtswissenschaft* 5:4 (1940), pp. 267–78, reprinted in *Staat, Großraum, Nomos*, ed. Günter Maschke (Berlin: Duncker & Humblot, 1995), pp. 372–87, at p. 372.

been translated throughout as "law of peoples" to allow readers to interpret Schmitt's notion of this term as something potentially quite different from the notions of international law prevalent in the 1940s or those notions of international law prevalent today.

# Acknowledgments

I am thankful for the thoughtful generosity of Victoria Kahn and Jane O. Newman who placed me in contact with the editors and publisher of *Telos*, Russell Berman, Timothy Luke, David Pan, Maria Piccone, and Robert Richardson, for and with whom it has been a delight and an honor to work on this translation and edition.

For helpful readings and corrections of earlier versions of this translation, introduction, and edition, I am thankful to David Bates, Russell Berman, Philip Bender, Maximiliane Berger, Andreas Eder, Ron Hassner, Eva Herzog, Kinch Hoekstra, Ellen Kennedy, Hannes Kerber, Raphael Magarik, John McCormick, Heinrich Meier, Pierre-Yves Modicom, Anne Norton, Thomas Oehl, Robert Richardson, Aaron Roberts, Ruth Starkman, Shannon Stimson, Lars Vinx, Joanna Williamson, and the anonymous reviewers for Telos Press.

I have been very fortunate to have many great teachers: Mark Bevir, Annabel Brett, Chris Brooke, Wendy Brown, James Forder, Timothy Hampton, Bob Hargrave, Robert Hass, Ron Hassner, Sudhir Hazareesingh, Kinch Hoekstra, Victoria Kahn, Noel Malcolm, Heinrich Meier, Stephen Mulhall, Diego Pirillo, John Robertson, Richard Serjeantson, Ethan Shagan, Shannon Stimson, Adam Swift, and Steve Weber. To Kinch Hoekstra and Shannon Stimson, I am especially grateful as teachers and mentors, for the privilege and delight of studying political philosophy and the history of political thought with them at Berkeley, during what have been, for me, the happiest of times.

I am thankful for the love of my family—my mother, Elizabeth, my sister, Ellie, and my dear friend and companion, Joanna.

My work on this translation and edition is dedicated to Professors Timothy Hampton, Kinch Hoekstra, Victoria Kahn, Jane O. Newman, and Shannon C. Stimson, with gratitude for their intellectual generosity and with admiration for their scholarship.

Samuel Garrett Zeitlin<br>
Berkeley, California<br>
June 2015

# Geography, Warfare, and the Critique of Liberalism in Carl Schmitt's *Land and Sea*

Russell A. Berman

Carl Schmitt has long been recognized as one of the most important German legal and political theorists of the twentieth century. His reception in recent decades in the English-speaking world and elsewhere approaches that of other major thinkers—Theodor Adorno, Walter Benjamin, and Jürgen Habermas—who have all become crucial points of reference in contemporary cultural and theoretical debates. Schmitt's prominence is curious, however, given his notorious association with the Nazi regime and his anti-Semitism: hardly an auspicious beginning for an intellectual-historical afterlife. This problem is particularly acute in *Land and Sea* (1942) because one of its central symbols, the Leviathan, draws on both Thomas Hobbes and, as Schmitt emphasizes, a particular Jewish source. (Schmitt had recently discussed this material in his 1938 volume *The Leviathan in the State Theory of Thomas Hobbes: Meaning and Failure of a Political Symbol*.)

The network of allusions and images in *Land and Sea* begins to unfold fairly conventionally: the first section includes a nearly obligatory Goethe quotation, followed in the next by a quartet of pre-Socratics: Thales, Heraclitus, Anaximenes, and Empedocles. Those reference points stage a cultural-conservative self-understanding in play since the Romantics, namely, Germany as heir to ancient Greece. Nietzsche had similarly insisted on a subterranean continuity between the Dionysian force of ancient Greek tragedy and the cultural eruption he believed he had found in the operas of Richard Wagner. In the Nazi era, one could point to the opening, nearly surrealistic sequence in Leni Riefenstahl's film *Olympia*, which establishes a direct genealogy between the ruins of Greek antiquity and the modernity of the Olympic Games in Berlin in 1936. The examples of this Greco-German cultural affinity are legion but therefore also thoroughly expected. What is unexpected is the presentation in section 3 of *Land and Sea*, where Schmitt abruptly turns to Jewish imagery.

The central argument in *Land and Sea* involves fundamental tensions between land-based and sea-based cultures. For Schmitt, this binary provides a vehicle with which to capture historical and contemporary political conflicts, but it also serves as a paradigm with which he can ground his analysis in elemental forces. The antagonism between land and sea, between terrestrial and maritime cultures, is symbolized by the existential struggle between two beasts: "For ages, the elementary opposition between land and sea has been noted, and still near the end of the nineteenth century it was a beloved image to depict the tensions of the time between Russia and England as the battle of a bear with a whale-fish." In this comment from section 3, Schmitt seems at first glance to be doing little more than glossing a political cartoon, although the two countries chosen, we will discover, represent antagonistic existential modalities: land mass versus oceans. His point, however, is to push ahead to the core of the myth and to name its putative Jewish source: "The whale-fish is the great, mythic fish, the Leviathan,...the bear one of many symbolic representatives of land animals. According to medieval interpretations of the so-called Kabbalists, world history is a battle between the powerful whale-fish, the Leviathan, and the equally strong land animal, the Behemoth, which is imagined as a bull or as an elephant." Each of the two alternative types of polities, maritime

England and terrestrial Russia, derives genealogically from a totemic animal, meaning that the political theory of *Land and Sea* ultimately depends on a mythology, the origin of which Schmitt makes absolutely clear to any reader who might not understand the Kabbalistic reference: "Both names, Leviathan and Behemoth, stem from the Book of Job (chapters 40 and 41)." Schmitt goes on further to underscore the Jewish origins, even naming the variant of the myth treated by the well-known nineteenth-century German-Jewish poet Heinrich Heine (well known but officially shunned under National Socialism). To be sure, the more emphatically Jewish the association, the more Schmitt, in an anti-Semitic gesture of his own, gives the account a cruel twist, turning it nearly into a blood-libel. Details on this treacherous rhetoric are richly available in the copious notes to this edition, prepared by Samuel Zeitlin.

The Jewish source for the essay, the battle-unto-death between Leviathan and Behemoth, provides the mythic core, profoundly elemental and at the same unmistakably political and contemporary: "Now, the Kabbalists say that the Behemoth exerts itself to rip apart the Leviathan with its horns or teeth, while the Leviathan, on the contrary, holds shut the mouth and nose of the land animal with its fins so that it cannot eat or breathe. This is, as descriptive as only a mythic image is capable of being, the sketch of the blockade of a land power by a sea power, which cuts off the land from supplies in order to starve it out. Thus do both fighting powers mutually kill each other." Behemoth versus Leviathan: land versus sea, Russia versus England in the nineteenth century or, more importantly, in Schmitt's 1940s, Germany versus Anglo-America as the mythic repetition of the irrepressible conflict between terrestrial and maritime worlds, between the order and stability of solid earth and its chaotic, disorderly, and threateningly anarchic opposite, the sea.

International conflicts therefore derive ultimately from a prior antinomy embedded in the very character of the planet: earth and water, land and sea. While this binary underpins Schmitt's argument, it is not, ultimately, a matter of a symmetrical opposition of two equal sides. On the contrary, from the outset of the essay, Schmitt makes it clear that humanity has a privileged relationship to the earth. We are "land-dwellers," we are naturally at home on dry land, and we consequently use the term "the earth" as the designation we give to our planet, "although, with respect to the extent of its surface, it is known to be almost three quarters water and only one quarter earth, and, indeed, the largest pieces of earth within it only swim like islands." Should we alternatively—this is his sly, rhetorical suggestion—name our planet "the water"? Of course not: for even though most of the planet is covered with oceans, we treat the earth, not the water, as our genuine home, and our cultures reflect the existential condition of having firm ground beneath our feet. Or more precisely: this terrestrial character applies in most but not all cases, for there are exceptions, those peoples who live otherwise and spend their lives and pursue their livelihood on the waters. Schmitt mentions "autothalassic" peoples living in the maritime niches of the South Seas, as well as the whalers who venture out into the great oceans (he dwells on *Moby Dick* and praises Melville, who, in his words, "is for the world's oceans what Homer is for the eastern Mediterranean"). These examples of life on the sea may seem to be only minor exceptions, marginal cases in the history of land-based humanity, but in terms of the overall argument, they establish an opening that is crucial. They enable Schmitt to turn his gaze away from the normative case of earth-bound cultures in order to examine the pull of the oceans, an undertow that generates profound changes in cultures that choose maritime destinies. Within the constraints of the essay, he offers a sketch of a civilizational history that not only accounts for the long trajectory of seafaring but moreover explores the conflicts between nations and cultures, between those rooted deeply in a place and its limitations, and others drawn to the sea, its expansiveness, instability, and lack of confinement.

In this "world-historical meditation," Schmitt evokes the confrontation between the seafaring ancient Greeks and the "many-domained," land-based Persians, as well as the antagonism between Carthage, defined by Mediterranean trade, and Rome, "an Italian republic of peasant farmers and a pure land power." The account reviews the lineage of defining sea battles as well, for Schmitt the decisive turning points in world history: Salamis (480 BC), Actium (30 BC), Lepanto (1571), and the defeat of the Spanish Armada (1588). Much in this narrative is necessarily abbreviated and only suggestive, but the contrast between his characterizations of Venice and England is especially telling. Both figure as sea-based forces, but in quite different ways. For Schmitt, Venice stands as the most prominent maritime power of the medieval world, a direct beneficiary of the Crusades. With its rise "a new mythic name is called into the great history of the world. For almost half a millennium the republic of Venice was seen as the symbol of dominion of the sea and of wealth founded on sea trade." Given this maritime character, Schmitt even argues that Venice anticipated features of the England that would emerge after its own later, decisive turn to the sea: "the great wealth; the diplomatic superiority, with which the sea power knew how to exploit the oppositions between the land powers and to conduct its wars through others; the aristocratic constitution, which appeared to have solved the problem of internal political order; the toleration with respect to religious and philosophical opinions; the asylum for liberal ideas and for political emigration." All these Venetian features, so Schmitt argues, foreshadow oceanic

England, and it is striking to what extent Schmitt betrays a profound admiration for this profile, especially because he offers an explicit political decoding: Venice, like England, was the home of an intellectual and political liberalism, which is otherwise the characteristic target of Schmitt's acerbic criticism.

However, this posited similarity between Venice and England undergoes an important relativization—the two cases are similar but hardly identical—in a way that bears on important differences in their respective relations to the sea and that also reflects Schmitt's own political agenda. He illustrates the Venetian maritime character with a poetic invocation of the *sposalizio del mare*, the marriage with the sea, an annual ritual during which the doge (and today still the mayor of Venice, albeit with more modest appointments) sails into the sea beyond Lido to drop a ring into the water and recite "Desponsamus te, mare, in signum veri perpetuique domini" ("We wed thee, sea, in the sign of the true and everlasting Lord"). The mythic enactment established and staged the Venetians' bond to the waters; or, in Schmitt's words, "The Venetians themselves, their neighbors, and peoples from far off saw in this a persuasive symbol, which gave a mythic consecration to sea-born power and sea-born wealth." Yet as much as the nuptial ceremony, with all its pomp and beauty, celebrated the link between city and sea, Schmitt also points out that the very core of this myth, the marriage, implies a non-identity, since the two distinct actors joining together to share a common destiny maintain their own heterogeneous characters. Urban Venice turns to the sea, but does not become one with it: "the ceremony allows for the distinct recognition that the symbolic act does not receive its sense from an elementary maritime existence; here, rather, a highly developed coastal and lagoon culture created for itself its own particular style of festive symbols. Mere navigation of the sea and a culture erected upon the exploitation of an advantageous coastal position is indeed something other than resituating a complete historical existence from the land to the sea as into another element."

Coastal Venice engages with the sea and traverses it, although Schmitt deprecates this mastery as "mere navigation." The alternative, which he locates in England, involves something much more radical (or rather: something much more liberal, in Schmitt's sense), the "resituating of a complete historical existence from the land to the sea," an elemental metamorphosis. Before we explore this English alternative more carefully, a full redefinition of the culture in maritime terms, let us take note of the literary strategies, the contrast between the dazzling splendor of the Venetian *sposalizio* and the symbolism with which Schmitt embodies maritime England. The scene now shifts, in section 8, to the reign of Elizabeth and the transformation of a society of sheep herders and wool traders into a center of piracy and "corsair capitalism," marked by widespread participation "in the great business of loot." In place of the medieval merchants of Venice, Schmitt's England is populated by predatory buccaneers, an ideal type exemplified by the Killigrew family of Cornwall, which produced generations of pirates. A rhetorical feature of this passage stands out: Schmitt's repetitive use of the term "elite" in his introduction to a colorful description of the piracy: "From their way of life and their world image we receive a more lively and more correct picture of the then leading classes and the true 'elite,' than from official reports"; and then again, "Let us linger a moment with this highly interesting elite." While a historical characterization of early modern England remains Schmitt's ostensible concern, he also obviously gives vent to a pique against the English ruling class as such: the rulers are only pirates, and the self-important "elite" is no elite at all, but merely criminal. Such are the sentiments of a German nationalist in the midst of the Second

World War. The contrast he conveys is this: Venetians marry the sea, while the English plunder foreign ships.

Yet Schmitt goes far beyond a denunciation of piracy in order to suggest a broad reshaping of English culture and society during the early modern period. While the Venetians, representatives of a coastal culture, pledge their love to the sea in a marriage ceremony, the English, in his account, undergo a fundamental cultural transformation through a comprehensive internalization of maritime existence. The crux of this shift is a "spatial revolution," a radical change in the understanding and experience of space. The world historian Schmitt prefaces his account of English modernity by recounting the reorganizations of space under Alexander, the Roman Empire, and through the Crusades, and he dwells especially on the impacts of early modern arts and science, including perspective in Renaissance painting and Copernicus's remapping of the skies. Both restructure the European sense of space, as does the conquest of the Americas with extensive economic and legal consequences. However, it is the transformation of England's self-understanding and her claim on global space that is the center of Schmitt's argument. He spells out the profound significance of "the British appropriation of the sea" in section 16: "The notion that a land power could exercise world power encompassing the whole globe was, according to [the English] worldview, unheard of and unbearable. It was otherwise for a world dominion that was established on a maritime existence separated from the land and which encompassed the oceans of the world." England's redefinition as a maritime existence forms the basis of its global hegemonic claims. It is worth noting how the original asymmetry of *Land and Sea* is reversed here. Schmitt began the essay by grounding the human condition on land, while noting the exceptions of water-based cultures: land is properly prior to sea. Yet maritime modernity inverts this order. After its turn toward the oceans, England—in Schmitt's view—assumes that it is appropriate to exercise a global hegemony because it is a sea-based power, although it would not countenance similar ambitions for a land-based power: recall the earlier discussion of the conflict between Leviathan and Behemoth as one between sea and land, England and Russia.

Schmitt certainly intends to highlight the hypocrisy that he identifies in the political position he projects onto England: the claim that no power should exercise hegemony, except for a sea-based power like herself. The accusation is in effect a version of familiar criticisms of liberal regimes of free trade, according to which formal freedom and generalized rules merely mask particular interests. Yet beneath the political dispute, Schmitt also names an existential and elemental problem. Venice married the sea, but remained apart from it, while England, in Schmitt's account, has submitted to a thoroughgoing reinvention of its culture, its laws, and its self-understanding in the spirit of the maritime turn. "A small island on the northwest coast of Europe became the midpoint of a world empire by turning away from solid land and deciding for the sea. In a purely maritime existence, it found the means of a world-dominion spread over the entire earth. After the separation of land and sea and the cleft of both elements had become the basic law of the planet, on this basis there arose a powerful framework of doctrines, propositional arguments, and scientific systems, with which the wisdom and rationality of this condition was clarified, without recognizing the originary deed, the British appropriation of the sea and its time-bound character." Between the Elizabethan Age and the eighteenth century, modes of thinking and political practices came to pervade English culture, transforming what had been an island, but nonetheless part of Europe, into an island separate from the continent, pursuing its fate and identity in the world's oceans. Schmitt underscores the radicality of this change in the opening to section 17: "England is an island. However, only by first becoming the bearer and center of the elementary turn from the fixed land to the high sea, and only as the heiress of all the maritime energies released at that time, did it transform itself into the island, which is what one means when one ever and again intones that England is an island. And only in first becoming an island in a new, heretofore unknown sense did it complete the British maritime appropriation of the world oceans and complete the first phase of the planetary spatial revolution." This unique transformation of England as an ocean-defined culture soon had ripple effects, generating new phases of a rapidly spreading and increasingly abstract modernity. The narrative of England's maritime transformation is, in the end, a theory of modernization in spatial terms.

Schmitt describes this modernity—maritime, liberal modernity—in somber colors. A primary feature is the brutal appropriation of the territories of the western hemisphere, a violent and cruel process that Schmitt condemns. He describes how European peoples "swarmed out into these expansive spaces," where they "treated the non-European and non-Christian lands and peoples...like ownerless property, belonging to the first Europeans who took it in possession." At the foundation of the new regime, the new *nomos* of the world, lies this sort of acquisitive lawlessness, analogous to British piracy except on a much larger scale. Schmitt singles out Francisco di Vitoria for praise for defending the legal claims and rights of the indigenous populations in *De Indis* (1532). Schmitt, however, has a particular interest in exploring the political theologies behind the conquests, which he maps especially onto a competition between Catholicism and Calvinism. He locates continental Germany, with its land-bound Lutheranism, as only on the margins of this world-historical revolution, subject to its impacts and consequences but only indirectly implicated. This discussion is directly relevant to our contemporary interests in colonialism, imperialism, and the emergence of postcolonial perspectives.

The pessimistic account of the oceanic turn pertains as well to the conduct of warfare in general. The conquest of the Americas was so violent and genocidal not only because the adversaries were non-Christian and racially different but also—this is Schmitt's suggestion—because the nature of warfare under the sign of the sea undergoes an extreme brutalization. In conventional European warfare, land war primarily involved a conflict between the forces of opposing states. "Only the fighting hosts confront one another as enemies, while the non-fighting civilian population remains outside the hostilities. The civilian population is not an enemy and shall not be treated as an enemy, so long as it does not partake in battle." Fair enough, although there were certainly egregious exceptions. Nonetheless the distinction between civilian and military was, conceptually at least, easy to grasp in a terrestrial context. Once the conflict moves to the oceans, however, that stability disappears. For Schmitt, the ocean represents a space where borders are impossible or, at least, extremely difficulty to define, space is fluid and subject to motion, and the distinction between civilian and military targets grows blurry very rapidly. Of course, in principle, one can posit a neat distinction between merchant and military vessels; however, in the maritime context, the potential that the trading ship might ultimately contribute to the vitality of the war effort renders the difference hard to maintain. "For sea war, on the contrary, at its basis lies the thought that the trade and economy of the enemy ought to be targeted. The enemy in such a war is not only the fighting opponent but also every member of an enemy state, and finally also the neutral party conducting trade with the enemy and who stands in an economic relation with the enemy."

The blurring of the difference between commercial and military vessels echoes a broader theme in Schmitt and elsewhere in twentieth-century German thought, such as Hannah Arendt's concern with the rise of the social or Jürgen Habermas's argument concerning the contamination of the liberal public sphere by economic interests. The land war, in Schmitt's account, is political, in the sense that the military forces of the respective states confront each other, avoiding (or trying to avoid) the civilian population. In contrast the sea war begins with the premise that the enemy's economy is the proper target, i.e., at stake is a political (military) intrusion into the private sphere of economy that however simultaneously pulls the social world—civilian populations, including the indigenous groups of the new world—into warfare. "It is grounded in the essence of these typical means of sea war that they may be directed at combatants as well as non-combatants." In this way, warfare becomes, Schmitt suggests cynically, a venue of egalitarianism, with access to everyone. "In particular, a blockade aiming at starvation strikes, without distinction, the whole population of the blockaded domain, the military and civilian population, men and women, the elderly and children." Schmitt no doubt has in mind the expansion of warfare against civilian populations around him in 1942, the constraints on the economy, and the initial bombing of German cities by allied forces; at the same time, this expansion of violence against civilian populations also of course defined German military practice, especially in Eastern Europe and against targeted groups, above all the Jews. Indeed one can turn Schmitt's argument concerning sea warfare against Germany with regard to the role of submarines and civilian casualties in the First World War, in particular the sinking of the *Lusitania* in 1915, which contributed significantly to the American decision to enter the war and therefore ultimately to the German defeat.

In addition to imperialist aggrandizement in the western hemisphere and the emergence of indiscriminate warfare, Schmitt highlights one further ominous feature of maritime modernity. His argument has centered on the transformation of England from a poor and pastoral agricultural economy to the center of global maritime rule and trade. Yet treating the England of the eighteenth and nineteenth centuries, he can hardly ignore the impact of industrialization. "The Leviathan transformed itself from a great fish into a machine," we read in section 18, by which he means that England, the trading powerhouse, underwent the industrial revolution, which leads Schmitt to pose the question of technology and its relevance to the transformation of human culture. Given the topic of *Land and Sea*, he inquires specifically into the industrialization of seafaring. "The machine altered the relation of the humans to the sea." Gone are the adventurers, the brave sailors, and the whalers of yore. "The daring type of men, which the grandeur of sea power had effected up to this time, lost its old sense." Technology obviated the need for bravado, courage, and physical strength; where once sailors battled the ocean directly, machines took their place, profoundly changing the relationship to the elemental challenge. "A dominion over the sea erected upon mechanized industry is manifestly something other than a sea power, which is attained every day in the hardest unmediated battle with the element." The industrialization of the maritime character degrades the participants, leaving them only an alienated existence, which, for Schmitt, comes to characterize English society and culture as a whole. "The industrial revolution transformed the children of the sea born from the element of the sea into machine builders and machine attendants." That description of a degraded population stands as Schmitt's corollary to the earlier denunciation of the predatory elite: the ruling class is criminal and the working class servile. Upstairs, Downstairs: such is his England, for this wartime writer in Germany, but such as well is his estimation of liberalism and its consequences, behind the high principles of which he suspects elitism, hypocrisy, and alienation.

What are the political and analytic consequences of *Land and Sea*? The critique of England as the paradigmatic maritime state should be understood in the context of the Second World War, although it echoes standard anti-British sentiments from the First World War and even earlier. Werner Sombart famously encapsulated the conflict between England and Germany as one between *Händler und Helden* (*Merchants and Heroes*), the title of his 1915 volume. His antinomy of mercantile acquisitiveness and soldierly values shares much with Schmitt's binary: Leviathan and Behemoth, the seafaring world of international commerce in conflict with the solidity of the territorial state. By the end of Schmitt's reflections, moreover, the enemy has expanded from England to the United States or rather to the constellation of Anglo-America; it is 1942 after all. Despite its continental expansion, the United States represents, for Schmitt, the principle of the sea, where limitlessness implies both imperialist expansion and universalistic, democratic ethics, which are inherently inimical to any stable order. In opposition to them stand models of legitimate sovereignty, defined borders, and social hierarchy within a people. The landscape of categories here is largely consistent with ideas Schmitt had been articulating for decades, in particular in *The Crisis of Parliamentary Democracy* (1923) with its own critique of liberalism and Wilsonianism.

However, one might imagine turning the tables on Schmitt. In place of his mapping the paradigms of maritime and terrestrial cultures onto England and Germany respectively, one could redeploy the analytic categories and turn them both toward Germany. This would defuse Schmitt's wartime agenda and instead represent an invitation to tease out competing currents within Germany history and society itself, one Germany open to the ocean and the other tied to the integrity of territorial regimes. That perspective directs us immediately to significant transitions marked, most dramatically and symbolically, by the dismissal of Bismarck in 1890 and Wilhelm II's pursuit of naval power that put imperial Germany in direct competition with England, one of the contributing factors leading to the First World War. At stake then is the conflict between a Bismarckian vision of Germany as a European power, within a continental balance, and the Kaiser's ambition to become a world power, be it through colonies, through naval capacity, or, ultimately, though nearly unlimited annexationist ambitions in the East. The categories of *Land and Sea*, by extension, can enrich discussions of cultural geography in German and Central European history more broadly: again and again, German *Westpolitik* has implied forms of integration into a liberal, Atlanticist community of states, while *Ostpolitik*, even under dramatically different regimes, pulled Germany further into the Eurasian land mass and toward Russia, the same Behemoth to which Schmitt refers as locked in conflict with Leviathan and the temptations of the sea.

Yet for the contemporary reader, the importance of *Land and Sea* does not lie only in Schmitt's own wartime polemics or in its symptomatic value as a document of German history—as important as each of those aspects certainly are. Rather, as with much of Schmitt's work, the attraction today involves his insights into liberalism, his concerns about the stability of state sovereignty, and deep-seated anxieties about forces of disorder that challenge the integrity of culture. The left reception of Schmitt can find in his work, and especially in this essay, a proleptic and powerful critique of neoliberalism, in the sense that the limitlessness of maritime culture can be taken to prefigure the autonomous expansionism of market society, oblivious to local prerogatives and *nomoi* and combining high principle with self-interestedness, not to mention predatory glee. That Schmitt himself incorporates, verbatim, an attack on European imperialism can make him even more appealing to progressive readers who would otherwise not want to accept the whole Schmitt package, least of all the tainted biography but perhaps not even the political theological paradigm. Whether the left Schmittians will accept his fundamentally conservative cultural criticism is unpredictable. Still it is difficult not to find in him a critique of alienation and a defense of local, particular cultural traditions threatened by the logic of unlimited expansionism. In that sense, *Land and Sea* could appeal to proponents of a conservative anti-imperialism generally opposed to any and all foreign interventions and therefore sometimes attacked as isolationism. Finally, there is a further aspect of the essay that can resonate with contemporary readers, a planetary materialism that grounds culture in the elements of the environment. *Land and Sea* is about nothing if not the human dependence on the natural world in which we live. Our existence is earth-bound, and while Schmitt does not anticipate the environmental crisis discourse of today, he certainly locates humanity emphatically in an environmental context. A bridge could be built from this planetary thinking to, for example, Martin Heidegger or Hans Jonas's advocacy of responsibility to the environment. Indeed one would not have to push Schmitt's account very far to extract from it the accusation that the abandonment of the soil in order to opt for the sea, which is to say, for the global market, itself represents a destructive disregard of the natural, earthly home.

In *Land and Sea* Schmitt stages a world-historical conflict between two principles, mapped onto two elements that stand in opposition to each other. Treating the essay as a document of German history and nationalist ideology, one can watch Schmitt use that oppositional structure in order to identify enemies: England, America, Jews. Beyond those particular political polemics, Schmitt also elaborates a broader conceptual account of the law of the land in conflict with the unlimited and emptied expanse of the sea. Schmitt tends to locate order in the former, anarchy in the latter. This short text can therefore also serve as a key to other strands in Schmitt's thought, his critique of liberalism, the defense of sovereignty, and his concerns with forces of disorder, including the disruptive impact of technology and the destruction of the environment. These aspects make *Land and Sea* a vital contribution to contemporary discussions of our political and planetary condition.

# Propaganda and Critique:
## An Introduction to *Land and Sea*
### Samuel Garrett Zeitlin

On the cover of the dust jacket of the 1981 edition of Carl Schmitt's *Land and Sea*, there is a circular emblem. In this drawing, encircled with a double line and a border of minute circles, one perceives a globe. The globe is poised upon a beach like a crystal ball upon a pedestal. On the globe's face, one can perceive the shapes of the continents of Africa, Asia, Australia, and Europe. North and South America are barely visible. This globe of the earth is itself positioned on a shore between the land, with several rocks and what seems to be a crustacean or a crawling lobster, and the sea, which is empty and vast. Across the sea, one can make out mountains as well as what looks like a human habitation—a house or a farm. These mountains appear to be another continent across the empty ocean, encompassing the globe on both its sides.[1]

The reader approaching *Land and Sea* and the cover of the 1981 edition of the work looks at the picture from the land out

1. Carl Schmitt, *Land und Meer: Eine weltgeschichtliche Betrachtung* (Cologne: Hohenheim/Edition Maschke, 1981), dust jacket, front cover. In a telephone conversation on July 27, 2015, with the editor of the 1981 edition, Günter Maschke related that he chose the image out of a book of sixteenth- and seventeenth-century emblems, and presented the image to Carl Schmitt, who approved the image for the front cover of the last edition of *Land and Sea* published in his lifetime. The editor of the 1981 edition related further that Schmitt found the image appealing and fitting for the work. Cf. Arthur Henkel and Albrecht Schöne, eds., *Emblemata: Handbuch zur Sinnbildkunst des XVI. und XVII. Jahrhunderts* (Stuttgart: Verlag J. B. Metzler, 1976), p. 727.

onto the sea, across the ocean. The cover image is perspectivally centered on the land, and the perspective of the frontispiece mirrors the claims that Schmitt advances in *Land and Sea* on behalf of his political anthropology. "You need only walk to the seashore and raise a glance and already the overwhelming surface of the sea encompasses your horizon," Schmitt writes in the first section of this work. "It is remarkable that the human, when he stands upon a shore, naturally gazes out from the land to the sea and not, conversely, from the sea to the land."[2]

In this way, in both its pictorial and textual facets, Schmitt's political anthropology presents itself as an apparent matter of reflective self-evidence. Those standing on the shore know to keep their feet upon the ground. Those staring at the 1981 cover of *Land and Sea* have the sea before them and the land behind and beneath them. Standing on the shore, the cover image implies, one is naturally cautious: one does not turn one's back to the ocean, exposing oneself to the dangerous and the unknown.

The historian and memoirist Nicolaus Sombart described *Land and Sea* as Carl Schmitt's "most beautiful book."[3] For Sombart, it was also Schmitt's "most important book,"[4] because "it contains *in nuce* the quintessence of his Gnostic philosophy of history."[5] Another scholar, writing a generation after Sombart,

2. Schmitt (1981), pp. 8–9; Schmitt (1954), p. 4; Schmitt (1942), p. 4. Schmitt, *Land and Sea*, section 1, p. 7, below.

3. Nicolaus Sombart, *Jugend in Berlin, 1933–1943: Ein Bericht* (Munich/Vienna: Carl Hanser Verlag, 1984), pp. 21, 255.

4. Ibid., p. 21: "Es war die Zeit, in der er sein vielleicht bedeutendstes, sicher aber sein schönstes Buch *Land und Meer* veröffentlicht." Cf. ibid., p. 255: "Er schrieb gerade, wie sich bald herausstellen sollte, an seinem Büchlein 'Land und Meer', sein, ich sagte es schon, schönstes Buch. Nein, ich bin sicher, auch sein wichtigstes Buch, denn es birgt in nuce die Quintessenz seiner gnostischen Geschichtsphilosophie."

5. Ibid., p. 255.

has claimed that *Land and Sea* reveals far more than Schmitt's views on questions of the philosophy of history: "*Land and Sea* is wide-ranging, encyclopaedic, poetic, and philosophically provocative. If there is a book that contains Schmitt's philosophy, it is this."[6]

Carl Schmitt's *Land and Sea* is a strange and haunting work. In it, anti-Jewish stereotypes coincide with lamentations against industrial whale hunting, while belles-lettristic odes to Herman Melville and Jules Michelet, political anthropology, and anti-British martial propaganda are interwoven into an ostensibly "world-historical" whole.

## Composition

Writing in the mid-1950s, close to the occasion of the publication of the second edition of *Land and Sea* in 1954, Carl Schmitt claimed that he conceived the argument of *Land and Sea* in the summer of 1940. In the 1954 "Sauerland"-Heft of the publication *Merian*, Schmitt described the origin of *Land and Sea* as follows:

> On a rainy holiday in the summer of 1940, my ten-year-old daughter bothered me to narrate something to her. I am not a good narrator. The juristic way of thinking and speaking, which has been transformed into blood and flesh within me, disrupts unreflective fable-making and transforms every beautiful story into a matter of fact or a state of affairs, into a *case*, and if it becomes particularly intense, into a criminal case. At the time I was occupied with questions concerning the maritime law of peoples [*Völkerrecht des Meeres*]. In order now to remain within the domain of my theme of the

---

6. Eduardo Mendieta, "*Land and Sea*," in Stephen Legg, ed., *Spatiality, Sovereignty and Carl Schmitt* (London: Routledge, 2011), pp. 260–67, at p. 260.

law of peoples and simultaneously to do the child's bidding, I began to speak of pirates and whale hunters. Unforeseen, I fell into the element of the sea, which up until then was foreign to me. The whole of world history opened itself suddenly under the new aspect of the opposition of the elements land and sea. From there surprising knowledge and insights disclosed themselves. Thus arose the little text *Land and Sea: A World-Historical Meditation*, which appeared in Reclams-Universal-Bibliothek and shall again shortly be printed there anew.[7]

In temporal accord with Schmitt's self-presentation of his inspiration for writing *Land and Sea*, yet absent from this postwar reminiscence, are the series of articles in which Schmitt sketched and drafted *Land and Sea*, published in 1940 and 1941 in the Nazi weekly *Das Reich*,[8] which a contemporary historian has described as the "favourite propaganda vehicle" of Joseph Goebbels.[9] Writing for the March 9, 1941, issue of *Das Reich*,

---

7. Carl Schmitt, "Welt großartigster Spannung," in *Staat, Großraum, Nomos*, ed. Günter Maschke (Berlin: Duncker & Humblot, 1995), pp. 513–17, at p. 513; cf. Günter Maschke, "Anhang des Herausgebers," in ibid., p. 517; Joshua Derman, "Carl Schmitt on Land and Sea," *History of European Ideas* 37, no. 2 (2011), pp. 181–89, at p. 181: "Within a year's time, the topic of his children's story had become an *idée fixe*."

8. Joseph W. Bendersky, *Carl Schmitt: Theorist for the Reich* (Princeton, NJ: Princeton Univ. Press, 1983), p. 261n59; Franco Volpi, "Il potere degli elementi," in Carl Schmitt, *Terra e Mare: Una riflessione sulla storia del mondo*, trans. Giovanni Gurisatti (Milan: Adelphi Editore, 2011 [2002]), pp. 113–49, at pp. 125n1, 147.

9. Mark Mazower, *Hitler's Empire: Nazi Rule in Occupied Europe* (London: Penguin, 2009 [2008]), ch. 17, p. 553. Cf. Richard J. Evans, *The Third Reich at War: How the Nazis Led Germany from Conquest to Disaster* (London: Penguin, 2009 [2008]), ch. 3, p. 246: "The Propaganda Minister coupled this with repeated press reporting of alleged atrocities committed against German soldiers by troops of the Red Army. The message was clear: the Jews were conspiring across the world to exterminate the Germans; self-defence demanded that they be killed wherever they were found. In response to the

Schmitt claimed that "It pertains to the oldest stock of human historical interpretation to behold in the opposition between sea powers and land powers a motor and the main content of world history. The wars between Athens and Sparta, Carthage and Rome are the famous examples from classical history."[10] Yet, in this article, "Das Meer gegen das Land," Schmitt did not content himself with classical historical examples. "Popular comparisons," Schmitt wrote,

> relate the battle of the whale-fish with the bear, mythic images of the great fish, the Leviathan, which battles with the great land animal, the Behemoth, with a steer or an elephant. Jewish Kabbalists of the Middle Ages—the worldly wise Abravanel among them—have given these depictions an important addition, in which they note that both great animals mutually slay one another, but the Jews regard the battle from a distance and eat the flesh of the slain beasts. The wars of England against the powers of the European continent—against Spain, France, and Germany, are often brought forward in this connection as well. Naturally, here there are many parallels.[11]

---

threat, as Goebbels declared on 20 July 1941 in an article for *The Reich*, a weekly journal he had founded in May 1940 and which had reached a circulation of 800,000 by this time, Germany and indeed Europe would deliver a blow to the Jews 'without pity and without mercy' that would bring about their ruin and downfall." Jeffrey Herf, *The Jewish Enemy: Nazi Propaganda During World War II and the Holocaust* (Cambridge, MA: The Belknap Press of Harvard Univ. Press, 2008 [2006]), p. 21: "*Das Reich* became the single most important journal read by the Nazified German political and intellectual establishment. It was a bellwether of Nazi policy and offered the propaganda minister a weekly platform from which he could reach both the Nazi faithful and a more sophisticated and politically astute readership than that of mass-circulation newspapers."

10. Carl Schmitt, "Das Meer gegen das Land," *Das Reich*, March 9, 1941, pp. 1–2, reprinted in *Staat, Großraum, Nomos*, pp. 395–400, at p. 395.

11. Ibid.

Schmitt's article, "The Sea against the Land," proceeded to draw these loose parallels, describing England as at once holding the power of the Leviathan over the world's oceans but also oriented by others in its imperial rule, as it was, in Schmitt's view, by one "Disraeli—an Abravanel of the nineteenth century"[12]— parallels that would recur, in some cases verbatim, in *Land and Sea*, upon publication late the following year.[13] Schmitt's article, published prior to American entry into the Second World War and prior to Hitler's breach of the Molotov-Ribbentrop Pact several months later, made no explicit mention of either America or Russia, instead directing what seems to be a blood libel against the Jewish people and prophesying the end of the British Empire: "It will soon become a historical memory, a mere episode in the great history of nations. And to our grandchildren we shall narrate the legend of the world empire of the Leviathan."[14]

Seven months prior, again writing in *Das Reich* in the aftermath of Dunkirk and the fall of the French Third Republic to Nazi occupation and Vichy, Schmitt had written of the potential of American entry into the war. In the September 29, 1940, issue of *Das Reich,* in an article entitled "The Spatial Revolution: From Total War to Total Peace" ("Die Raumrevolution: Durch den totalen Krieg zu einem totalen Frieden"), Schmitt presented America as still facing a choice about how to comport itself in relation to the war then raging in Europe. "Here the question arises," Schmitt speculated in the pages of *Das Reich*, "as to which front the other Anglo-Saxon power, the United States

---

12. Schmitt, "Das Meer gegen das Land," pp. 1–2, in *Staat, Großraum, Nomos*, p. 397.

13. Cf. sections 3 and 17 of Schmitt, *Land and Sea*, pp. 11–16, 81–83, below.

14. Schmitt, "Das Meer gegen das Land," pp. 1–2, in *Staat, Großraum, Nomos*, p. 398.

of America, will side with."[15] Again, in "The Spatial Revolution," Schmitt made no mention of Russia or the Soviet Union; the question of Germany's war efforts were directed westward toward Britain and the question of U.S. entry into the war.

A year later, on October 16, 1941, Schmitt delivered an early lecture version of *Land and Sea* to a meeting organized by the Institut Allemand, directed by Karl Epting in occupied Paris.[16] In a diary entry dated "Paris, October 18, 1941," Ernst Jünger wrote: "Midday in the 'Ritz' with Carl Schmitt, who had held a lecture the day before yesterday on the significance of the distinction between land and sea in the law of peoples.... Conversation on the academic and literary controversies of our time. Carl Schmitt compared his situation to that of...the captain in Melville's 'Benito Cereno' and in this connection cited the maxim: '*Non possum scribere contra eum, qui potest proscribere*' ['It is not possible to write against the one who is able to dictate death']."[17]

15. Carl Schmitt, "Die Raumrevolution: Durch den totalen Krieg zu einem totalen Frieden," *Das Reich*, September 29, 1940, reprinted in *Staat, Großraum, Nomos*, pp. 388–94, at p. 391. According to the editor of the Schmitt-Jünger correspondence, Helmuth Kiesel, in a letter to Schmitt dated October 2, 1940, in reference to this article, Jünger wrote: "Yesterday, I brought my wife your fine article [*Ihren schönen Aufsatz*] back from Berlin." Ernst Jünger–Carl Schmitt, *Briefe 1930–1983*, ed. Helmuth Kiesel, 2nd ed. (Stuttgart: Klett-Cotta, 2012 [1999]), pp. 106, 552.

16. The biographic sources differ with respect to the title of the lecture. Franco Volpi gives the title as "Die völkerrechtliche Bedeutung des Unterschiedes von Land und Meer," while Reinhard Mehring gives the title as "La mer contre la terre." The invitation from the Deutsche Institut/Institut Allemand prints the title of the lecture as "Staatliche Souveränität und Freies Meer" but announces that Schmitt will deliver the lecture in French. Letter of Schmitt to Ernst Jünger, September 24, 1941, in Jünger–Schmitt, *Briefe 1930–1983*, pp. 130–32, 567; Volpi, "Il potere degli elementi," p. 147; Reinhard Mehring, *Carl Schmitt: Aufstieg und Fall* (Munich: C. H. Beck, 2009), p. 410; cf. p. 473. Cf. Mazower, *Hitler's Empire*, p. 431.

17. Ernst Jünger, *Strahlungen I: Das erste Pariser Tagebuch*, in *Sämtliche Werke in Achtzehn Bänden*, Erste Abteilung, Tagebücher II, Band 2 (Stuttgart:

On Jünger's presentation in his diary, by late 1941, during the period of his public lectures on land and sea, Schmitt was frustrated by his inability to write openly against those with the power to proscribe. If Jünger's account is accurate, whom might Schmitt have had in mind as holding the power to proscribe in 1941? What might Schmitt have wished to say that the power of proscription prevented?

## Schmitt and the Molotov–Ribbentrop Pact

As several scholars have noted, Schmitt did not take a low view of the Molotov–Ribbentrop Pact or its successor treaties for the parceling out of Eastern Europe between Nazi Germany and the Soviet Union.[18] Writing in early 1941 in the third edition of his pamphlet *Völkerrechtliche Großraumordnung*, Schmitt praised "the German–Russian friendship and border treaty of September 28, 1939," for its use of the term *Reich*. The treaty formed Schmitt's principal example of an international legal document that deployed *Reich* as the basic unit of *Völkerrecht*, or the law of peoples, which Schmitt identified with the Roman legal tradition of the *ius gentium*.[19] The pact legislated the basic principle of "non-intervention of spatially foreign powers" into the affairs of either *Reich* (the German *Reich* or the

---

Klett-Cotta, 1979 [1949]), p. 265; cf. Bendersky, *Carl Schmitt*, p. 262 and 262n64.

18. Timothy Nunan, "Notes on the Text" prefacing his translation of *Völkerrechtliche Großraumordnung*, in Carl Schmitt, *Writings on War*, ed. Timothy Nunan (Cambridge: Polity Press, 2011), pp. 75–76; Gopal Balakrishnan, *The Enemy: An Intellectual Portrait of Carl Schmitt* (London: Verso, 2000), pp. 238–45.

19. Carl Schmitt, *Völkerrechtliche Großraumordnung mit Interventionsverbot für raumfremde Mächte: Ein Beitrag zum Reichsbegriff im Völkerrecht* (Dritte, unveränderte Auflage der Ausgabe von 1941) (Berlin: Duncker & Humblot, 2009 [1941]), pp. 47–48; Schmitt, *Writings on War*, pp. 100–1. Cf. Victor Zaslavsky, *Class Cleansing: The Massacre at Katyn*, trans. Kizer Walker (New York: Telos Press Publishing, 2008), p. 82.

Soviet *Reich*) as a valid principle (*geltendes Prinzip*) of the law of nations.[20] For Schmitt, writing in 1941, the legal agreement between Hitler and Stalin was not only valid treaty law; it was also a valid source of legitimacy for understanding *Reiche* as the basic units of the law of peoples and the legal source of the (in Schmitt's view) valid principle for a *Reich* holding sway within its own "great space," or *Großraum*. For Schmitt, the Molotov-Ribbentrop Pact and successor pacts offered legal support to both Hitler's geopolitics of *Lebensraum* imperialism and Schmitt's own *Großraum* nationalist expansionism.

Schmitt continued to assert the validity of the Hitler-Stalin agreements even after the treaties had been broken by the German invasion of Soviet territory that began on June 22, 1941. In a preface to the fourth edition of his *Völkerrechtliche Großraumordnung*, which Schmitt dated July 28, 1941, Schmitt noted that he had expanded the work by an entire chapter and made other "small improvements."[21] However, Schmitt retained the passage on the validity of "the German-Russian friendship and border treaty of September 28, 1939."[22] More than a month into the Hitlerian invasion of the Soviet Union,[23] Schmitt was

20. Schmitt, *Völkerrechtliche Großraumordnung*, pp. 47-48.
21. Ibid., p. 9; Schmitt, *Writings on War*, p. 76.
22. Ibid., pp. 47-48; Schmitt, *Writings on War*, pp. 100-1. Cf. Nunan, "Notes on the Text," p. 75: "The fourth and final edition of *The* Großraum *Order of International Law*, which was published in the summer of 1941, included a final new section on 'The Concept of Space in Jurisprudence' and retained the paragraph on the German-Soviet Treaty, even though the German *Reich* had already invaded the Soviet Union shortly before the publication of the fourth edition. Schmitt added a preliminary remark, written on July 28, 1941, to this version of the text that comments obliquely on this fact."
23. Cf. Dirk van Laak, "Von Alfred T. Mahan zu Carl Schmitt: Das Verhältnis von Land- und Seemacht," in Irene Diekmann, Peter Krüger, and Julius H. Schoeps, eds., *Geopolitik: Grenzgänge im Zeitgeist* (Potsdam: Verlag für Berlin-Brandenburg, 2000), Band 1.1, pp. 257-82, at p. 273: "Lange Zeit wollte Hitler durch einen Verzicht auf koloniale und maritime Politik Großbritannien zu einem Bündnis mit Deutschland bewegen, um freie Hand für

asserting in print that the successor agreements to the Molotov–Ribbentrop Pact were still valid law, and thus that Operation Barbarossa was a violation of the law of nations.[24] For Schmitt's international thought, the Hitlerian invasion of the Soviet Union was an international crime in a way that the Hitlerian invasions of Czechoslovakia, Austria, Denmark, Poland, Belgium, and France were not. It was also a geopolitical mistake, from Schmitt's perspective, in a way in which the prior invasions had not been.[25] Where Schmitt had praised his Führer in

---

seine Absicht zu erhalten, Deutschland als führende kontinentale Weltmacht zu etablieren. Letztlich mag er kalkuliert haben, der Weg nach Afrika werde über Moskau führen." (Tr. "For a long time Hitler wanted to move Great Britain into an alliance with Germany via [German] renunciation of colonial and maritime policy, in order to gain a free hand for his aim of establishing Germany as the leading continental world power. Finally he [Hitler] may have calculated that the way to Africa would be reached via Moscow.")

24. In the period 1939–42, Schmitt also supervised a dissertation on the legal implications of the Hitler–Stalin pact at the University of Berlin—a dissertation that he passed in May 1942, almost a year after the treaty had been broken by Operation Barbarossa. Cf. Mehring, *Carl Schmitt: Aufstieg und Fall*, pp. 402–3, 686n50.

25. Sombart, in his memoirs, recounts the following conversation with Schmitt after the Nazi invasion of the Soviet Union: "Ever and again he [Carl Schmitt] posed the question to himself (and me): What is this for a war in which we are engaged? This war which is to me so curiously distant and indifferent! Did it have any sense at all after the defeat of Poland and France? The revision of the Versailles Diktat, that was Hitler's historical mission. Those were conventional land wars. But now? What should one think of this? In the East we are conducting an ideological war of annihilation, in the West a worldwide sea war. We simply aren't up to this." ("Immer wieder stellte er sich (und mir) die Frage: Was ist das für ein Krieg, in den wir da verwickelt sind? Dieser Krieg, der mir so seltsam und gleichgültig war! Hatte er nach der Niederwerfung Polens und Frankreichs überhaupt noch einen Sinn? Die Revision des Versailler Diktates, das war Hitlers historischer Auftrag. Das waren konventionelle Landkriege. Aber jetzt? Was sollte man davon halten? Im Osten führen wir einen ideologischen Vernichtungskrieg, im Westen einen weltweiten Seekrieg. Dem sind wir überhaupt nicht gewachsen.") Sombart, *Jugend in Berlin*, p. 266. Julien Freund, in his introduction to the

print on numerous occasions,[26] he retained his print position on the legal validity of the Molotov–Ribbentrop Pact and its successor conventions even as *Blitzkrieg* advanced through the Ukraine and the Eurasian steppe and as Nazi soldiers advanced on Moscow.[27]

---

1985 French translation of *Land and Sea*, reports Schmitt speaking similarly of Hitler's conquests: "In order to understand these explanations by Schmitt, it is convenient, I believe, to recall another conversation. 'One has asked you,' I said to him once, 'to write a work on Hitler. While tempted by this offer, in the end you rejected it. I would like to know what idea you have of this man.' All of a sudden, Schmitt's response surprised me: 'The strategic errors of Hitler were the result, in the first instance, of political blindness.... Like almost the totality of the intellectuals of the epoch, Hitler, too, was the adversary of the Treaty of Versailles. His true, perhaps his only, political goal was the abrogation of this Treaty. Hitler had marched on Paris in June 1940 for this sole end and, having attained it, didn't know what to do politically." ("Pour bien comprendre ces explications de Schmitt, il convient, je crois, de les compléter par une autre conversation. 'On vous a demandé, lui dis-je une fois, d'écrire un ouvrage sur Hitler. D'abord tenté par cette offre, vous l'avez en fin de compte rejetée. J'aimerais savoir quelle idée vous vous faites de cet homme.' Sur le coup, la réponse de Schmitt me surprit: 'Les erreurs stratégiques d'Hitler furent au premier chef un aveuglement politique.... Comme la quasi totalité des intellectuels de cette époque, Hitler fut lui aus[s]i l'adversaire du Traité de Versailles. Son véritable, peut-être son seul but politique, fut l'abrogation de ce Traité. Hitler a marché sur Paris en juin 1940 à cette seule fin et, l'ayant atteinte, ne sut plus que faire politiquement.'") Julien Freund, "Introduction," in Carl Schmitt, *Terre et mer: Un point de vue sur l'histoire mondiale*, trans. Jean-Louis Pesteil (Paris: Éditions du Labyrinthe, 1985), pp. 9–16, at pp. 14–15.

26. Yves Charles Zarka, *Un détail nazi dans la pensée de Carl Schmitt* (Paris: Presses Universitaires de France, 2005), pp. 53–88.

27. Evans, *The Third Reich at War*, p. 179: "In the first week of the invasion, Army Group Centre broke decisively through Soviet defences, encircling the Red Army troops in a series of battles. It had already taken 600,000 prisoners by the end of the second week in July. By this time, more than 3,000 Soviet artillery pieces and 6,000 tanks had been captured or destroyed, or simply abandoned by the troops. 89 out of 164 divisions in the Red Army had been put out of action. German forces took Smolensk and pushed on towards Moscow."

### The Human

The first words of *Land and Sea* are "the human" (*der Mensch*), and it is worth dwelling, for a moment, on what Schmitt understands by "the human" and what he is doing, politically and theoretically, with this term. In Schmitt's view, not all members of the species *homo sapiens* qualify for the Schmittian class of "the human." "The human," Schmitt claims in the opening sentence of this work, is a land-being (*Landwesen*), a land animal, a land-dweller who moves upon the firmly grounded earth.[28] As Schmitt asserts throughout *Land and Sea*, not all members of the species *homo sapiens* are land-beings, land animals, or land-dwellers in Schmitt's understanding of these terms.

In all the editions of *Land and Sea* published in his lifetime, Schmitt claims that "On the isles of the South Sea, in the Polynesian seafarers, Canaks and Sawoiori, one recognizes still the last remnants of such fish-humans [*Fischmenschen*]."[29] While Schmitt has relegated some to the status of "fish-humans [*Fischmenschen*],"[30] the English, according to Schmitt, are simply "fish,"[31] and there are others who are even less fortunate.

---

28. Schmitt (1981), p. 7; Schmitt, *Land and Sea*, section 1, p. 5, below.
29. Schmitt, *Land and Sea*, section 1, p. 8, below. Schmitt (1981), p. 10; Schmitt (1954), p. 5; Schmitt (1942), p. 6: "Auf den Inseln der Südsee, bei polynesischen Seefahrern, Kanaken und Sawoiori, erkennt man noch die letzten Reste solcher Fischmenschen." Cf. Schmitt's letter to Ernst Jünger, dated August 16, 1941, in Jünger–Schmitt, *Briefe 1930–1983*, p. 125: "Die 'autothalattischen' zum Unterschied von 'autochthonen' Rassen (Polynesier als Rasse solcher 'Autothalatten') sprechen nur in Vokalen; das bezeichnet der Autor als typisch für eine nicht landtretende, reine Meer- und Fisch-Menschenrasse."
30. Schmitt (1981), p. 10; Schmitt (1954), p. 5; Schmitt (1942), p. 6.
31. Schmitt (1981), p. 92.

Schmitt's notion of "the human" seems to find its place in a series of binary oppositions:

| | | |
|---|---|---|
| Earth (element) | vs. | Water (element) |
| Soil (*Boden*) | vs. | Ocean |
| Land | vs. | Sea |
| Land peoples (*Landvölker*) | vs. | Sea peoples (*Seevölker*) |
| Land war (*Landkrieg*) | vs. | Sea war (*Seekrieg*) |
| Land-oriented existence | vs. | Maritime existence |
| The Human (*der Mensch*) | vs. | Fish, Sea dogs |
| Behemoth | vs. | Leviathan |
| Germany, Russia, Italy | vs. | England, America |

Although this series of oppositions breaks down and is modified at various points in Schmitt's text,[32] the notion of landed peoplehood as criterion for "the human" is deployed by Schmitt as a political weapon with polemical aims. As other scholars have noted,[33] Schmitt's notion of "the human" is a privative category—denying the humanity of those who are excluded from it.

In several places in his text, Schmitt claims that the decision of English seafarers for a "purely maritime existence" coincided with their transformation into *Seeschäumer* (frothing sea dogs) or "fish."[34] The choice for the sea over and against the land is, in the terms of *Land and Sea*, a chosen forfeiture

---

32. Especially in section 17, Schmitt (1981), pp. 92–93.
33. Ellen Kennedy, "*Hostis* Not *Inimicus*: Toward a Theory of the Public in the Work of Carl Schmitt," in David Dyzenhaus, ed., *Law as Politics: Carl Schmitt's Critique of Liberalism* (Durham, NC: Duke Univ. Press, 1998), pp. 92–108, at p. 94: For Schmitt, Kennedy argues, humanity "is a polemical word that negates its opposite."
34. Schmitt (1981), p. 92; Schmitt, *Land and Sea*, section 17, p. 79, below.

of one's humanity that occasions a transformation into something other than human.

While, in Schmitt's presentation, it is the English decision for the sea that occasions a forfeiture of their human status, Schmitt deploys his criterion of landedness to polemically dehumanize the Jewish people, independent of such a decision. In Schmitt's presentation, the Jewish people, lacking a land and the corresponding ability to dwell in the land, also lack the status of being human.[35] Humans, for Schmitt, are land-dwellers who, in their "pure" form, are peasant farmers who live in farm houses.[36] Jews, for Schmitt in 1942, are landless wanderers who live in tents.[37]

---

35. Schmitt (1942), pp. 9–10; Schmitt (1954), pp. 8–9; Schmitt (1981), pp. 16–17; Schmitt, *Land and Sea*, section 3, pp. 11–16, below.

36. Schmitt, *Land and Sea*, sections 1 and 3, below. Cf. Schmitt, *Dialogue on New Space* (*Gespräch über den Neuen Raum* [1955/1958]), section 4: "[Altmann:] House and property, marriage, family and hereditary right, all that is built upon the foundation of a terrestrial mode of being [*eines terranen Daseins*], in particular that of the agricultural farm. The farmer, too, as we call him, takes his name not from the work of farming or from tilling the field. The farmer is named after the farm, which is to say the farm house, which belongs to him and to which he belongs. Thus, at the core of a terrestrial existence there stands the house." Carl Schmitt, *Dialogues on Power and Space*, trans. Samuel Garrett Zeitlin (Cambridge: Polity Press, 2015), p. 73. Cf. Jacob Taubes, *Ad Carl Schmitt: Gegenstrebige Fügung* (Berlin: Merve, 1987), section 1.

37. Schmitt (1942), p. 10: "So töten sich, meinen diese Juden, die beiden kämpfenden Mächte gegenseitig. Die Juden aber, sagen sie weiter, stehen daneben und sehen dem Kampfe zu. Sie essen das Fleisch der sich gegenseitig tötenden Tiere, ziehen ihnen die Haut ab, bauen sich aus dem Fell schöne Zelte und feiern ein festliches, tausendjähriges Gastmahl. So deuten die Juden die Weltgeschichte." ("Thus, these Jews claim, both the fighting powers mutually kill one another. The Jews, however, they say further, stand back and behold the battle [as spectators]. They eat the flesh of the beasts who mutually kill each other, remove the skin, and from the hide build themselves fine tents and celebrate a festive, millennial feast. Thus do the Jews interpret world history.") Cf. van Laak, "Von Alfred T. Mahan zu Carl Schmitt," p. 278.

In the 1942 text of *Land and Sea*, Schmitt's notion of "the human" excludes both the Jewish people and the British, but it does not exclude the Russians or Italians. Russia, throughout *Land and Sea*, is identified as a land power, like Germany.[38] In Schmitt's presentation, Russian fur hunters are to Siberia what English whale hunters are to the world's oceans.[39] Where Russia is figured by Schmitt as a land power, and, thus, as a natural ally of Germany, Japan is acknowledged to be an island, like Britain.[40] Schmitt concedes that not all islands are alike, especially with respect to making a political decision for a maritime existence, however his explicit acknowledgment that Japan is an island raises the question of Schmitt's view of the advisability of alliances outside the German "*Großraum*" of continental Europe,[41] and whether, in Schmitt's view, Germany's alliance with Japan was a geopolitical error. "Land powers," in Schmitt's vocabulary in *Land and Sea*, are anthropologically identified with peoples who base their existence on the land. In connecting Germany and Russia through a shared humanity, which,

38. Schmitt (1942), pp. 9, 23, 69; Schmitt (1954), pp. 8, 19, 57; Schmitt (1981), pp. 16, 35, 97. Schmitt, *Land and Sea*, sections 3, 5, 18, below.

39. Schmitt, *Land and Sea*, section 5, p. 31, below. Schmitt (1942), p. 23; Schmitt (1954), p. 19; Schmitt (1981), p. 35.

40. Schmitt, *Land and Sea*, section 17, pp. 76–77, below.

41. At least as late as 1936, Schmitt was asserting in print that according to "racial theory [*Rassenlehre*]," as he understood this term, Germany's future allies were "Non-Aryans." Carl Schmitt, *Das Judentum in der Rechtswissenschaft, Die deutsche Rechtswissenschaft im Kampf gegen den jüdischen Geist* (Berlin: Deutscher Rechtsverlag, 1936), pp. 14–17, at p. 16: "We owe to racial theory [*Rassenlehre*] the distinction between the Jews and other peoples. The French, the English, and the Italians have exercised great influence upon us. Within this there are good and evil influences. But there always is in such an influence of Aryan peoples something fully other than the influence of the Jewish spirit. We are speaking here, where the concern is the Jews, not, in general, of 'Non-Aryans.' Thereby the Jew is placed into a society, in which he finds unexpected allies and quite possibly may advance arm in arm with grand samurais and knightly Magyars."

in Schmitt's view Germans do not share with the English, the Americans, and the Jewish people, Schmitt may seem to subtly imply that the annulment of the Hitler–Stalin Pact was a geopolitical error for Nazism.

## The Pirate and the Capitalist Corsair

In Roman law and in the *ius gentium*, which Schmitt identified with *Völkerrecht*, piracy is defined with reference to a specific notion of enmity. The pirate, as Schmitt was well aware, is legally defined as a *hostis generis humani*, as the enemy of humankind.[42] In his writings in the 1930s and 1940s, Schmitt was attuned to American and British attempts during and after the First World War to define the attacks of German U-boats upon American and British commercial vessels as acts of piracy, and thus as acts inimical to humanity.[43] To this end,

---

42. Carl Schmitt, "Der Begriff der Piraterie (1937)," in *Positionen und Begriffe im Kampf mit Weimar—Genf—Versailles 1923-1939*, 4th rev. ed. (Berlin: Duncker & Humblot, 2014 [1940]), pp. 274–77, at p. 274: "Nach der alten, auch anläßlich dieser Konferenz oft wiederholten Formel gilt der Pirat als 'Feind des Menschengeschlechts,' hostis generis humani." (Tr. "According to the old, also on the occasion of this conference often repeated formula the pirate is held to be the 'enemy of humankind,' *hostis generis humani*.") Cf. Carl Schmitt, *Die Wendung zum diskriminierenden Kriegsbegriff*, 4th ed. (Berlin: Duncker & Humblot, 2007 [1938]), p. 57n56: "Wilson hat in seiner Rede vom 2. April 1917 den Ausdruck 'Piraterie' zwar nicht gebraucht, wohl aber den deutschen Unterseebootkrieg als einen 'gegen die Menschheit' geführten Krieg bezeichnet, der ein 'Krieg gegen alle Nationen' sei. Damit war Deutschland mit den für die Piraterie üblichen Formulierungen zum hostis generis humani erklärt." (Tr. "In his address of April 2, 1917, Wilson did not deploy the term 'piracy,' but did indeed label the German U-boat war as war waged 'against humanity,' as a 'war against all nations.' With this, Germany was defined with the formulation normally used for piracy as the *hostis generis humani*.") Cf. Daniel Heller-Roazen, *The Enemy of All: Piracy and the Law of Nations* (New York: Zone Books, 2009), esp. pp. 16–22, 142–46, 163–170.

43. Schmitt, "Der Begriff der Piraterie (1937)," pp. 276–77; p. 277: "Sollte sich die englische Auffassung der U-Boot-Piraterie als ein allgemeiner

Schmitt followed closely the international negotiations related to the London Protocol, the London Naval Treaty of 1930, and the Nyon Arrangement, international protocols that attempted to fix the status of submarine attacks on commercial vessels as violations of the law of nations, often in terms that the *ius gentium* had reserved for acts of piracy.[44]

In *Land and Sea*, it is not German U-boats but the English people as a whole who are demarcated as pirates,[45] with

---

Völkerrechtsbegriff durchsetzen, so hätte der Begriff der Piraterie seinen Platz im System des Völkerrechts gewechselt. Er wäre aus dem leeren Raum unpolitischer Nichtstaatlichkeit in jenen für das Völkerrecht der Nachkriegszeit typischen Raum der Zwischenbegriffe zwischen Krieg und Frieden verlegt worden." (Tr. "Should the English conception of U-boat piracy have been established as a general concept in the law of peoples, thus the concept of piracy would have altered its place in the system of the law of peoples. It would have been removed from the empty space of unpolitical non-statehood into the space of concepts intermediate between war and peace typical for the law of peoples of the post-war period.") Cf. Schmitt, *Die Wendung zum diskriminierenden Kriegsbegriff*, pp. 13, 51, 57n56; Schmitt, *Writings on War*, pp. 218n178, 36, 68, 73; Heller-Roazen, *The Enemy of All*, pp. 226n38–39; letter of Ernst Jünger to Schmitt, dated November 3, 1937, in Jünger–Schmitt, *Briefe 1930–1983*, p. 68.

44. Heller-Roazen, *The Enemy of All*, pp. 137–46; Schmitt, "Der Begriff der Piraterie (1937)," pp. 274–77; cf. Schmitt, *Writings on War*, p. 218n178.

45. In a conversation with Schmitt from the period in which Schmitt was at work writing *Land and Sea*, Nicolaus Sombart recounts in his memoirs Schmitt speaking of the English people as follows: "The island England suddenly breaks off from the land and becomes a ship, which sails out upon the ocean. 'A ship,' he said furtively, 'a pirate ship.' The island England and its world-conquering seafaring required neither the absolute monarchy nor a standing land army, nor a fixed legal system, such as became a necessity for continental Europe. Reflectively he added: 'The English people simply didn't need a state, and nonetheless became a world power.... The English people, you see, had decided against the state—for the *free sea*!' 'We are land dwellers, Nicolaus,' he said, while we stomped through the Märkisch sand in Grunewald.... 'We can't even grasp what that means: the free sea!'" ("Die Insel England löst sich plötzlich vom Lande ab und wird zu einem Schiff, das auf die Ozeane hinausfahrt. 'Ein Schiff,' sagte er geheimnisvoll, 'ein Piratenschiff.' Die Insel England und ihre welt-eroberdende Seefahrt bedurfte weder

Schmitt claiming that the English turn to a maritime existence "transformed a people of shepherds into pirates."[46] Schmitt's redescription of the English as pirates is in keeping with his classification of the English as a *Seevolk*, and rhetorically turns the whole English people into *hostes generis humani*—thus manipulating the concept of piracy against those who would deploy it against the Germans and U-boat warfare.[47]

As we have seen, Schmitt's account of piracy in *Land and Sea* is partially a polemic turn of the concept of piracy against the English. In addition, it might be read as Schmitt's engagement both with Marx's account of primitive accumulation and

---

der absoluten Monarchie noch eines stehenden Landheeres, noch eines gesetzlichen Rechtssystems, wie es für das kontinentale Europa zu einer Notwendigkeit wurde. Nachdenklich fügte er hinzu: 'Das englische Volk hatte einen Staat einfach nicht nötig, und wurde trotzdem Weltmacht.... Das englische Volk, verstehst du, hat sich gegen den Staat entschieden—für das *freie Meer!*' 'Wir sind Landtreter, Nikolaus,' sagte er, während wir durch den märkischen Sand im Grünewald stapften, und stieß unwillig mit dem Stock auf.' Wir können gar nicht begreifen, was das heißt: das freie Meer!'" Cf. Sombart, *Jugend in Berlin*, p. 256.

46. Schmitt, *Land and Sea*, section 18, below; cf. ibid., sections 7 and 8.

47. In a conversation with Schmitt from the period in which Schmitt was at work writing *Land and Sea*, Nicolaus Sombart recounts in his memoirs Schmitt speaking of pirates as follows: "From the perspective of the Anglo-Saxon rule of the seas, we [Germans] are pirates—*hostes generis humani*, enemies of humanity. Pirate, as you already know, this is not the individual sea robber, but rather the ship and its entire crew, from the captain to the last cabin boy. Should the ship be captured, all would be hanged—imprisoned together, hung together—with the exception of those prisoners lying in chains. Here pardon will not be granted..." (ellipsis in the original) ("Aus der Perspektive der angelsächsischen Seeherrschaft sind wir Piraten—hostes generis humani, Feinde der Menschheit. Pirat, das weißt du schon, ist nicht der einzelne Seeräuber, sondern das Schiff und seine ganze Mannschaft, vom Kapitän bis zum letzten Kajütenjungen. Wird das Schiff gekapert, werden alle aufgehängt—mitgefangen, mitgehangen—mit Ausnahme der in den Ketten liegenden Gefangenen. Pardon wird da nicht gegeben..."). Sombart, *Jugend in Berlin*, p. 266.

with Max Weber's account of the Protestant ethic that frames the spirit of capitalism.

For Schmitt in *Land and Sea*, early modern piracy is intimately linked to Protestantism, so much so that he at times seems to claim that early modern piracy is *exclusively* Protestant: "All these Rochellois, Sea Beggars, and Buccaneers had a political enemy, namely, the Catholic world power of Spain," Schmitt writes. "As long as they held something of themselves, they fundamentally only captured Catholic ships, and saw this as work pleasing to God, as work blessed by God. They thus stood in a great world-historical front of what was then World Protestantism against what was then World Catholicism."[48] What, for Schmitt, links the pirate to the Protestant? What distinguishes a pirate from a soldier—a piratical fleet from a naval armada—is that a pirate is primarily not recognized by the governing authorities.[49] A pirate is fully outside the legal order, and in this respect importantly linked to Protestants, who were not originally recognized by the governing authorities or the governing churches.

In Schmitt's discussion of the "Protestant" character of piracy, one may recall Schmitt's indebtedness to Weber, to whose posthumous *Erinnerungsgabe* Schmitt contributed a reprint of three of the four chapters of his *Political Theology*.[50] Weber had linked capitalist mentalities to Protestant notions of

48. Schmitt, *Land and Sea*, section 7, p. 38, below.
49. Cf. Julien Freund, "Postface: La thalassopolitique," in Schmitt, *Terre et mer* (1985), pp. 91–121, at p. 108.
50. Heinrich Meier, *Die Lehre Carl Schmitts: Vier Kapitel zur Unterscheidung Politischer Theologie und Politischer Philosophie* (Stuttgart-Weimar: Verlag J. B. Metzler, 2009 [1994]), pp. 56n12–57n12; Reinhard Mehring, *Carl Schmitt: A Biography*, trans. Daniel Steuer (Cambridge: Polity Press, 2014), pp. 106–10; Mehring, *Carl Schmitt: Aufstieg und Fall*, pp. 124–29; Helmuth Kiesel, "Kommentar," in Jünger–Schmitt, *Briefe 1930–1983*, pp. 463–906, at pp. 660–61.

calling, grace, and asceticism—spiritual habits that encouraged saving and the formation of capital stock.[51] In Schmitt's presentation in *Land and Sea*, the Protestant ethic that gives rise to capitalism has very little to do with asceticism or the saving power of grace. The spirit of capitalism, in Schmitt's view, is driven by a Protestant ethic of piracy and plunder, particularly piracy and plunder against Catholic vessels transporting loot from the newly conquered Americas.

In *Land and Sea*, Schmitt's picture of the birth of early modern piracy is linked both to Protestantism—the pirate stands in a "great world-historical front of what was then World Protestantism"—but also with the history of legal recognition of pirates as corsairs and, in Schmitt's view, with the origin of capital accumulation.

Piracy, on account of its use-value, can under certain circumstances become recognized by a regal or princely government. The corsair is a recognized and authorized pirate, bearing a state-sanctioned letter of marque and reprisal from his government. In Schmitt's presentation in *Land and Sea*, the historical role of the corsair is substantial:

> the corsairs of the sixteenth and seventeenth centuries play a great historical role. They stand as active fighters in the grand world-historical confrontation between England and Spain. When they were caught, they were marked and hung as common criminals and thieving murderers by their enemies, the Spanish. Even their own government let them fall in cold blood when they became incommodious or when the cautions of external politics demanded it. Often, it was really an accident whether such a corsair ended as a bearer of regal honors or ended on the gallows as a pirate condemned to death. In addition, the different labels, like pirate,

---

51. Max Weber, *Die protestantische Ethik und der Geist des Kapitalismus*, ed. Dirk Kaesler (Munich: C. H. Beck, 2013 [1920]), pp. 96–202.

> corsair, privateers, merchant-adventurer,[52] were, in practice, unclearly and interchangeably deployed. Seen juristically, there is a great distinction between pirates and corsairs. The corsair has, in contrast with the pirate, a legal title, an empowerment from his government, a formal letter of marque and reprisal from his king. He may fly the flag of his country. By contrast, the pirate sails without legal mandate. For him, only the black pirate flag is appropriate. But as fine and clear as this distinction may be in theory, it dissolves in practice. The corsairs often overstepped the bounds of their mandates and sailed with false letters of marque and reprisal, sometimes also with forged letters of empowerment from non-existing governments.[53]

Schmitt's account of the recognition of the pirate (figured, by Schmitt, as a Protestant) may be meant as a parallel to the recognition of Protestants by regal and princely Protestant state churches in the sixteenth and seventeenth centuries. On Schmitt's account, the state-recognized pirate remains a pirate, albeit one who may sail under the recognized flag of his monarch or prince.

Schmitt explicitly links his account of the corsair, an agent of "World Protestantism," to capitalism: the pirate becomes a corsair, and the corsair becomes a corsair capitalist. Schmitt narrates this process as occurring in the reign of Queen Elizabeth I:

> Queen Elizabeth is freely held as the great founder of English rule of the seas, and this fame is also well-deserved. She began the battle with the Catholic world power of Spain. Under her government, the Spanish Armada was vanquished in the channel (1588); she honored and encouraged sea heroes like

---

52. In Schmitt's text "privateers" and "merchant-adventurer" are English in the German original.

53. Schmitt, *Land and Sea*, section 7, pp. 37–38, below.

Francis Drake and Walter Raleigh; from her hand the English East India Company, which later conquered all of India for England, received its trading privilege in the year 1600. In the forty-five years of her government (1558 to 1603), England became a rich country, which it had not been previously. Previously, the English had herded sheep and sold the wool to Flanders; now, however, the fabled loot of English corsairs and pirates flowed from all seas to the English island. The Queen rejoiced in these treasures and enriched herself with them. In this respect, in all her virginal innocence, she did nothing other than what numerous noble and bourgeois Englishmen and Englishwomen of her time did. They all took part in the great business of loot. Hundreds and thousands of Englishmen and Englishwomen at that time became "corsair capitalists."[54]

Schmitt's account of English imperial expansion and his subsequent account of the Killigrew family and "corsair capitalism" may be read as Schmitt's counter-narrative to Marx's discussion of "primitive" accumulation (*die sogenannte ursprüngliche Akkumulation*) in volume 1 of *Das Kapital*.[55] In both Schmitt's and Marx's accounts, capitalism is of English origin and proceeds from the expropriation of land people (*Expropriation des Landvolks*):[56] in Marx, the English peasant-farmers; in Schmitt, the conquistadors of the Catholic world powers Portugal and Spain.

---

54. "Corsair capitalists" is English in Schmitt's German original with partial German orthography, and preceded by a German translation of the term in quotation marks ("zu 'Korsaren-Kapitalisten,' zu corsairs capitalists"). Schmitt, *Land and Sea*, section 8, pp. 39–40, below.

55. Karl Marx, *Das Kapital: Kritik der politischen Ökonomie: Erster Band*, 40th ed. (Berlin: Karl Dietz Verlag, 2013 [1867]), ch. 24, "Die sogenannte ursprüngliche Akkumulation," pp. 741–91. Cf. Balakrishnan, *The Enemy*, pp. 241–42.

56. Marx, *Das Kapital*, ch. 24, "Die sogenannte ursprüngliche Akkumulation," sect. 2, "Expropriation des Landvolks von Grund und Boden," p. 744.

## Carl Schmitt on "Islam"

Carl Schmitt expresses his views on "Islam" at greater length in *Land and Sea* than perhaps in any other book that he published during his lifetime.[57] The Dark Ages, in Schmitt's view, are not attributable to the world-historical victory of Christianity. On the contrary, in Schmitt's opinion, "The fall of the Roman Empire, the expansion of Islam, the invasions of the Arabs and of the Turks brought about a centuries-long spatial darkening and land confinement in Europe."[58] Given the effects that he attributes to "the expansion of Islam," Schmitt praises the Byzantine Empire in *Land and Sea* for the achievement of holding back and forestalling the progress of "Islam." The Byzantine Empire, in Schmitt's understanding, was "a true 'forestaller,' a 'Katechon,' as one calls it in Greek; it 'held out,' despite its weakness, for many centuries against Islam and thereby hindered the Arabs from conquering all of Italy. Otherwise, as it transpired at the time with North Africa under the extinction of the ancient Christian culture, Italy would have been incorporated into the Islamic world."[59] Elsewhere in *Land and Sea*, Schmitt speaks in praise of the Battle of Lepanto, remarking that "Here, the Spanish-Venetian fleet collided together with the Turkish

---

57. Schmitt's 1950 treatise *Der Nomos der Erde* treats this theme at roughly equally length in the course of a larger work. Cf. Carl Schmitt, *The Nomos of the Earth in the International Law of the Jus Publicum Europaeum*, trans. G. L. Ulmen (New York: Telos Press, 2006 [2003]), pp. 53, 58, 65, 87, 112.

58. Schmitt (1981), p. 61. Schmitt, *Land and Sea*, section 11, p. 53, below.

59. Schmitt (1981), p. 19. Schmitt, *Land and Sea*, section 3, pp. 17–18, below. For further discussion of Schmitt's notion of the "Katechon," see Schmitt, *The Nomos of the Earth*, pp. 59–63, 87, 238. Cf. Tracy B. Strong, "Foreword: Carl Schmitt and Thomas Hobbes: Myth and Politics," in Carl Schmitt, *The Leviathan in the State Theory of Thomas Hobbes*, trans. George Schwab and Erna Hilfstein (Chicago: Univ. of Chicago Press, 2008), pp. vii–xxviii, at p. xxv; Balakrishnan, *The Enemy*, pp. 221–25; Meier, *Die Lehre Carl Schmitts*, pp. 243–49; Ruth Groh, *Carl Schmitts gnostischer Dualismus* (Berlin: LIT Verlag, 2014); 2 Thessalonians 2:6–7.

fleet and achieved the greatest sea victory that Christians have borne away from Mohammedans."[60] In the sweeping assessments of "Islam," "Arabs," and "Mohammedans," Schmitt may give voice to a broader anti-Semitism that extends beyond a virulent hatred of the Jewish people.[61]

In addition, Schmitt's political vocabulary of choice for his discussions of "Islam" in *Land and Sea* raises broader geopolitical questions. At the time of Schmitt's composition of *Land and Sea*, the National Socialists were engaged in expansive war beyond the so-called German *Großraum* in the Middle East and Northern Africa, and in coordinated activities with the Muslim Brotherhood in Egypt and with the Grand Mufti of Jerusalem in Mandate Palestine.[62] In *Land and Sea*, Schmitt admits that within the juristic frame of the "community of the Christian-European peoples" with which he is particularly concerned in its battle against adversaries (real or imagined), "the deployment of non-Europeans, Mohammedans, or Indians, as overt or covert aids or even as allies was never a cause of concern."[63] Applied to National Socialist policy in the Middle East in the period 1941–42, the thought that "deploying" "Mohammedans…as overt or covert aids" is not a cause of concern might seem to be Schmitt's endorsement of the Nazi alliance with the Muslim Brotherhood and the Grand Mufti to achieve the mutual Nazi aims of subverting the British Empire and destroying the Jewish people. On the other hand, Schmitt's sharp rhetoric in 1942 against both "Islam" and "Mohammedans"

60. Schmitt (1981), p. 27. Schmitt, *Land and Sea*, section 4, p. 24, below.
61. Cf. Strong, "Foreword: Carl Schmitt and Thomas Hobbes," p. xv.
62. David Motadel, *Islam and Nazi Germany's War* (Cambridge, MA: The Belknap Press of Harvard Univ. Press, 2014); Jeffrey Herf, *Nazi Propaganda for the Arab World* (New Haven, CT: Yale Univ. Press, 2010 [2009]); Matthias Küntzel, *Jihad and Jew-Hatred; Islamism, Nazism and the Roots of 9/11* (New York: Telos Press, 2009 [2007]), pp. 24–48.
63. Schmitt (1981), p. 74. Schmitt, *Land and Sea*, section 13, pp. 62–64, below.

may indicate a view that even National Socialist expansionism has its limits and that certain confessional alliances, such as the Nazi entanglement with the Grand Mufti, may be culturally ill-favored.[64] With respect to his rhetoric on "Islam" and "the deployment of...Mohammedans" against Nazism's mutual enemies, Schmitt may be caught in deep-seated cultural contradictions, which may reflect more deeply contradictory desires.

## Visions and Revisions:
## 1954 and 1981 Editions of *Land and Sea*

Writing for the 1954 "Sauerland"-Heft of *Merian*, Schmitt anticipated the second edition of *Land and Sea* as a new printing of his 1942 work.[65] Despite this presentation,[66] the 1954 edition of *Land and Sea* differed from its 1942 predecessor in several important respects. In the first instance, the 1954 edition omitted the "Overview" (*Überblick*) that had functioned as a summary table of contents in the 1942 edition, and which is reprinted below as an appendix to the current edition. In its place, in the 1981 edition, which follows the post–World War II 1954 edition in most respects, Schmitt added a brief afterword contrasting his reading of Hegel's *Elements of the Philosophy of Right* with the reading offered by "Marxism."[67] Schmitt first quotes from Hegel's treatise, "As the earth, fixed *ground* and

64. On the importance of culture for Schmitt, see David Pan and Russell A. Berman, "Introduction," *Telos* 142 (Spring 2008), pp. 3–6, at p. 3: "Culture precedes politics, life precedes law, theology precedes order."

65. Schmitt, "Welt großartigster Spannung," p. 513. Cf. Maschke, "Anhang des Herausgebers," p. 517; and Derman, "Carl Schmitt on Land and Sea," pp. 181–89.

66. The 1954 edition is itself presented as newly looked over—a new edition ("Neue, durchgesehene Auflage") on its title page; see Schmitt (1954), title page. Schmitt presents the work as a new printing in Schmitt, "Welt großartigster Spannung," p. 513.

67. Schmitt, *Land and Sea*, "Afterword," p. 95, below. Reinhard Mehring attributes the omission of the "Overview" (*Überblick*) to editorial forgetfulness

*soil*, is the condition for the principle of family life, so for industry the outward enlivening element is the sea," and then offers a somewhat brief and rather cryptic commentary: "I leave it to the attentive reader to find in my exertions the beginning of an attempt to bring to fulfilment this § 247 in a way similar to that in which §§ 243–246 was brought to fulfilment in Marxism."[68] By drawing attention to the soil (*Boden*) as "the principle of family life," Schmitt's 1981 afterword may construct a certain rhetorical parallelism—an epanaleptic construction—with the dedication of the work, "*Narrated to my daughter Anima*." In the 1981 edition, *Land and Sea* both begins and ends with reference to the family—a site of both inclusion and exclusion—a social unit, in Schmitt's presentation, situated on the dubious ground of blood ties and soil, of *Blut und Boden*.

In the 1942 edition of *Land and Sea* there is only a single footnote, which considers variant readings of the Latin in Seneca's tragedy *Medea*.[69] In the 1954 edition, Schmitt added a second footnote, linking the work of *Land and Sea* to his 1950 treatise, *The* Nomos *of the Earth*.[70] In keeping with this explicit

---

on the part of Schmitt's publisher, Reclam. Cf. Mehring, *Carl Schmitt: Aufstieg und Fall*, p. 702n106.

68. Ibid.

69. Ibid., section 11, below.

70. Ibid., section 13, note 90, below: "The Greek noun *Nomos* comes from the Greek verb *Nemein* and like this it has three meanings. *Nemein* is, in the first instance, the same as: to take, to appropriate (Nehmen). Consequently *Nomos* means in the first instance: appropriation (die Nahme). As in Greek, e.g., *Legein-Logos* is parallel to the German for to speak/speech [language] (Sprechen-Sprache), similarly the Greek: *Nemein-Nomos* is parallel to the German for to appropriate/appropriation (Nehmen-Nahme). Appropriation is in the first instance land-appropriation, later sea-appropriation as well, of which much has been said in our world-historical meditation, and in the domain of industry, industrial appropriation, i.e., seizing the industrial means of production. Second, *Nemein* means: partition and distribution [*Teilen und Verteilen*] of that which has been taken. *Nomos* is thus second: the fundamental partition and distribution of the soil and the order of

tie to the argument of *The* Nomos *of the Earth*, in editing the 1954 edition of *Land and Sea* Schmitt changes the temporal frame of his description of the "*nomos* of the earth." In the 1942 edition, Schmitt wrote: "The order of the firm land consists in its division into state dominions; the high sea is free, i.e., state-free and subject to the authority of no state dominion. These are the basic spatial facts, out of which the Christian-European law of peoples developed in the last three hundred years. This is the basic law, the *nomos* of the earth in this epoch."[71] In the 1954 edition, Schmitt changed the last sentence to "This *was* the basic law, the *nomos* of the earth in this epoch."[72] In 1954, the "Christian-European law of peoples" is a thing of the past, which, in Schmitt's view, it had not been in 1942.

No less strikingly, in the 1954 and 1981 editions, Schmitt plays down several of the passages directed against the war conduct of the British in the Second World War. Discussing the tactic of naval blockades in the 1942 edition of *Land and Sea*, Schmitt offered the opinion that in the blockade "the English disposition sees—because death by starvation is a bloodless

---

property which touches upon it. The third meaning is: to pasture (*Weiden*), i.e., using, economizing, and valuing of the soil derived from its partition, production, and consumption. Appropriating-Partitioning-Pasturing (*Nehmen-Teilen-Weiden*) are, in this sequence, the three fundamental concepts of any concrete order. Further on the meaning of *Nomos* in the book: *The Nomos of the Earth* (Cologne, 1950). (Second Edition, Berlin, 1974)."

71. Schmitt (1942), p. 60. Cf. Schmitt, *Land and Sea,* section 16, below.

72. Schmitt (1954), p. 50; Schmitt (1981), p. 86. Cf. Schmitt, *Land and Sea,* section 16, below. In the 1942 edition of Schmitt's text, this sentence reads: "This *is* the basic law, the nomos of the earth in this epoch" (emphasis added). In the 1954 edition, Schmitt altered this sentence by changing "is" (*ist*) to "was" (*war*), an alteration retained in the 1981 edition. Cf. Schmitt (1942), p. 60; Schmitt (1954), p. 50; Schmitt (1981), p. 86. In his *Dialogue on New Space* (*Gespräch über den neuen Raum* [1955/1958]), published in the year after Schmitt published the revised, 1954 edition of *Land and Sea*, Schmitt claims that atomic and hydrogen power obviated the spatial order of land and sea. Cf. Schmitt, *Dialogues on Power and Space*, pp. 63–64ff.

death—even a proof of higher humanity and refined humaneness, while to it the 'battle-based war' of continental warfare appears as cruel butchery."[73] Schmitt continued further in this vein in section 16 of *Land and Sea*: "This appeared to them good and self-evident; this is for them the same thing as civilization and humanity; it is peace and the law of peoples itself. What is most astounding is that other peoples [*Völker*] took over such English concepts as classical truths."[74] In the 1954 and 1981 editions, these passages on "the English disposition" were removed, even as Schmitt retained the passages in which he described the English as "fish" and as "a people of...pirates."

Perhaps most striking of all are Schmitt's revisions to his 1942 text related to his presentation of the Jewish people, whom Schmitt primarily refers to as "the Jews [*die Juden*]." In the 1942 edition, perhaps adhering to his 1936 pronouncement that all authors, scholars, and persons of Jewish origin should be marked as such[75] (which he retained in works published

73. Schmitt, *Land and Sea*, section 16. Schmitt (1942), p. 62; Schmitt (1954), p. 51; Schmitt (1981), p. 88; cf. Volpi, "Il potere degli elementi," p. 146.

74. Schmitt (1942), p. 62; Schmitt (1954), p. 52; Schmitt (1981), p. 89; cf. Volpi, "Il potere degli elementi," p. 146.

75. Carl Schmitt, "Die Deutsche Rechtswissenschaft im Kampf gegen den jüdischen Geist," *Deutsche Juristen-Zeitung* 40:20 (1936), pp. 1193–96; cited in Taubes, *Ad Carl Schmitt*, section 1; also cited in Heller-Roazen, *The Enemy of All*, pp. 226n53, 227n53. Cf. Mehring, *Carl Schmitt: Aufstieg und Fall*, pp. 372–78; Mehring, *Carl Schmitt: A Biography*, pp. 341–46. Schmitt, *Das Judentum in der Rechtswissenschaft, Die deutsche Rechtswissenschaft im Kampf gegen den jüdischen Geist*, p. 16: "We owe to racial theory [*Rassenlehre*] the distinction between the Jews and other peoples. The French, the English, and the Italians have exercised great influence upon us. Within this there are good and evil influences. But there always is in such an influence of Aryan peoples something fully other than the influence of the Jewish spirit. We are speaking here, where the concern is the Jews, not, in general, of 'Non-Aryans.' Thereby the Jew is placed into a society, in which he finds unexpected allies and quite possibly may advance arm in arm with grand samurais and knightly Magyars. Then he has the possibility to denounce the battle against the Jewish people as a battle against other non-Jewish peoples

in 1937,[76] 1938,[77] 1939,[78] 1940,[79] and 1941[80]), Schmitt was keen to refer to Benjamin Disraeli as "the Jewish politician Disraeli [*der jüdische Politiker Disraeli*],"[81] marking even one baptized into the Church of England as inescapably branded by descent. In the 1954 edition, as well as in the 1952 authorized Spanish

---

and set his German-inimical propaganda [*deutschfeindliche Propaganda*] under a new aspect. Finally, we are not speaking of the Jewish people as one of the 'National minorities.'... We are thus speaking of the Jews and calling them by their name."

76. Carl Schmitt, *The Turn to the Discriminating Concept of War (1937)*, in *Writings on War*, ed. Timothy Nunan (Cambridge: Polity Press, 2011), p. 40: "The relation this construction has with the teaching of social pluralism of the Jewish professor Laski (a professor teaching at the same London academy as Lauterpacht) ought to be at least mentioned, in spite of the fact that Laski, who has created the social theory of the Second International from the pragmatic philosophy of the true Anglo-Saxon William James, is not especially mentioned by Scelle in his own work."

77. Carl Schmitt, *The Leviathan in the State Theory of Thomas Hobbes: Meaning and Failure of a Political Symbol*, trans. George Schwab and Erna Hilfstein (Chicago: Univ. of Chicago Press, 2008 [1938]), p. 70: "Stahl-Jolson was the boldest in the Jewish front"; p. 69: "The nineteenth-century Jewish philosopher, Friedrich Julius Stahl-Jolson immediately recognized and utilized the gap"; p. 61: "the Jew, Moses Mendelssohn"; p. 23: "Of Jewish origin is apparently also the understanding of a contemporary of Hobbes, Isaac de la Peyrère, who exercised a great influence on Spinoza's critique of the belief in miracles."

78. Carl Schmitt, "Neutralität und Neutralisierungen (1939)," pp. 309–34 in *Positionen und Begriffe*, p. 334: "Auf dem Höhepunkt des preußischen Verfassungskonflikts hat ein jüdischer Abgeordneter, Dr. Eduard Simson... der Jude Simson."

79. Carl Schmitt, "Über die neuen Aufgaben der Verfassungsgeschichte," in *Positionen und Begriffe*, pp. 261–67, at p. 265: "Im Jahre 1890 war der Sieg des verfassungsrechtlichen Positivismus entschieden, dessen anerkannter Führer der jüdische Rechtsgelehrte Laband war."

80. Carl Schmitt, *The Großraum Order of International Law with a Ban on Intervention for Spatially Foreign Powers: A Contribution to the Concept of Reich in International Law (1939–1941)*, in *Writings on War*, pp. 75–124, at p. 108: "the most cited author for English pluralism, the Jew Laski."

81. Cf. Schmitt (1942), section 19, p. 72, with Schmitt (1954), section 19, p. 59.

translation published by the Instituto de Estudios Políticos in Madrid,[82] the emphatic moniker describing Disraeli as a *"Jewish politician"* was removed.[83] In the 1942 edition of *Land and Sea*, Schmitt further described Disraeli as "an initiate, an Elder of Zion [*ein Eingeweihter, ein Weiser von Zion*]"—deploying the term that in German corresponds to the forged *Protocols of the Elders of Zion*, a reference that fell from the 1954 German edition but which was retained in the 1952 translation that Schmitt authorized for publication in Franco's Spain.[84] In describing the battle between Behemoth and Leviathan in the 1942 edition, Schmitt wrote: "Thus, these Jews claim, both the fighting powers mutually kill one another. The Jews, however, they say further, stand back and behold the battle [as spectators]. They eat the flesh of the beasts who mutually kill each other, remove the skin, and from the hide build themselves fine tents and celebrate a festive, millennial feast. Thus do the Jews interpret world history."[85] In the 1954 German edition, this passage was altered to read as follows: "Thus do both fighting powers mutually kill each other. The Jews, however, these Kabbalists say further, then celebrate the festive millennial 'Feast

82. Carl Schmitt, *Tierra y Mar: Consideraciones sobre la Historia Universal*, trans. Rafael Fernandez-Quintanilla (Madrid: Instituto de Estudios Políticos, 1952), p. 107. On the Instituto de Estudios Políticos and its role in Schmitt's reception in Franco's Spain, see Jan-Werner Müller, *A Dangerous Mind: Carl Schmitt in Post-War European Thought* (New Haven, CT: Yale Univ. Press, 2003), pp. 270n6, 133–43.

83. Cf. Schmitt (1942), section 19, p. 72, with Schmitt (1954), section 19, p. 59; Schmitt, *Tierra y Mar* (1952), p. 107.

84. Schmitt (1942), p. 67; Schmitt (1954), p. 56; Schmitt (1981), p. 95; Raphael Gross, *Carl Schmitt und die Juden: Eine deutsche Rechtslehre* (Frankfurt am Main: Suhrkamp, 2005 [2000]), p. 276; Meier, *Die Lehre Carl Schmitts*, p. 238; Volpi, "Il potere degli elementi," p. 146. The 1942 version is retained in the 1952 Spanish translation by Fernandez-Quintanilla; Schmitt, *Tierra y Mar* (1952), p. 100.

85. Schmitt (1942), p. 10; Schmitt (1954), pp. 8–9; Gross, *Carl Schmitt und die Juden*, pp. 274–77; Meier, *Die Lehre Carl Schmitts*, pp. 237–40; Volpi, "Il potere degli elementi," p. 146.

of the Leviathan,' which Heinrich Heine narrated in a famous poem."[86] In the 1952 Spanish translation, the World War II-era version of these passages was retained.[87] Perhaps, for Schmitt in the early 1950s, certain markets (particularly those influenced by *Franquismo*) were regarded as more receptive to Schmitt's views on the Jewish people from 1942; views that, at root, it seems Schmitt did not alter.[88]

## The Elements of World History

In *Land and Sea*, Carl Schmitt gives voice to the opinion that the ancient doctrine of the four elements—earth, water, air, and

---

86. Schmitt (1942), p. 10; Schmitt (1954), pp. 8-9; Schmitt (1981), p. 17; Gross, *Carl Schmitt und die Juden*, pp. 274-77; Meier, *Die Lehre Carl Schmitts*, pp. 237-40; Volpi, "Il potere degli elementi," p. 146. In referring to Heine, Schmitt appears to refer to the terminal poem "Disputation," from the third section, *Hebräische Melodien* (*Hebraic Melodies*), of Heine's 1851 collection *Romanzero, Gedichte*. The passages that Schmitt removed from the 1942 edition and the passages that Schmitt retained in the 1954 and 1981 editions are missing in several respects from Heine's poem. First, Heine's "Disputation" makes no mention of Behemoth, and thus no mention of the battle between Behemoth and Leviathan, nor does he mention Jewish spectatorship of this battle. Second, Heine's "Disputation" makes no mention of the Jews skinning the Leviathan and using the hide of Leviathan to make tents, emphasized in Schmitt's 1942 edition. Third, in Heine's "Disputation" it is never mentioned who kills Leviathan, but, according to Heine's character Juda, it is God who offers the meat of the Leviathan to the chosen, the wise, and the just.

87. Schmitt, *Tierra y Mar* (1952), p. 17: "Así interpretan los judíos la historia universal."

88. Müller, *A Dangerous Mind*, pp. 133-43; Meier, *Die Lehre Carl Schmitts*, pp. 235-40. Cf. Taubes, *Ad Carl Schmitt*; Jacob Taubes, *Die Politische Theologie des Paulus* (Munich: Fink, 2003 [1993/1987]); Nicolaus Sombart, *Die deutschen Männer und ihre Feinde, Carl Schmitt—ein deutsches Schicksal zwischen Männerbund und Matriarchatsmythos* (Munich: Carl Hanser Verlag, 1991), esp. ch. 11, pp. 261-94; Bernd Rüthers, *Carl Schmitt im Dritten Reich: Wissenschaft als Zeitgeist-Verstärkung?* 2nd exp. ed. (Munich: C. H. Beck, 1990 [1989]), pp. 113-16. Reinhard Mehring claims that the alterations to the 1954 edition (preserved in the 1981 edition) were made at the behest of the publisher, Reclam. Cf. Mehring, *Carl Schmitt: Aufstieg und Fall*, pp. 474, 702n106.

fire—while "dissolved" by "modern natural science," nonetheless remains an "inextinguishably lively conception" and the meritorious basis for a world-historical meditation.[89] While Schmitt concedes that the doctrine of the four elements might raise problems in the domains of physics, metaphysics, and epistemology,[90] Schmitt maintains that "Nonetheless, for our historical meditation, we can stick with the four elements. For us, these elements are precisely simple and descriptive names. They are collective signifiers, which point to different grand possibilities of human existence. Therefore, we may still deploy them today and we may speak of land powers and sea powers in the sense of such elements."[91] On the basis of this elemental view, Schmitt asserts that "World history is a history of the battle of sea powers against land powers and of land powers against sea powers."[92] In Schmitt's view, world-historical battles are significantly those between Athens and Sparta, Carthage and Rome, England and Germany—and importantly *not* battles between Germany and Russia. Schmitt's construction of a human and humane, landed existence is elementally juxtaposed with a fishy and leviathanic maritime existence. Schmitt is concerned to present his notion of maritime existence in conjunction with a stadial view of maritime development. Drawing explicitly upon the theory of the nineteenth-century

89. Schmitt (1981), p. 12; Schmitt (1954), p. 6. Schmitt, *Land and Sea,* section 2, below.

90. Schmitt (1981), p. 13; Schmitt (1954), p. 6. Schmitt, *Land and Sea,* section 2, p. 9, below.

91. Schmitt (1981), p. 13; Schmitt (1954), p. 6. Schmitt, *Land and Sea,* section 2, pp. 9–10, below.

92. Schmitt (1981), p. 16; Schmitt (1954), p. 8. Schmitt, *Land and Sea,* section 3, p. 11, below. Cf. Schmitt (1981), p. 73; Schmitt (1954), pp. 42–43. Schmitt, *Land and Sea,* section 13, p. 63, below: "World history is a history of land-appropriations." Cf. David Armitage, "The Elephant and the Whale: Empires of Land and Sea," in *Journal of Maritime Research* 9, issue 1 (2007), pp. 23–36, at p. 28.

geographer Ernst Kapp,[93] Schmitt divides human relations with the element of the water into potamic, thalassic, and oceanic periods.[94] Describing Kapp's tripartite stadial view, which Schmitt himself subsequently adopts, Schmitt writes: "World history, for him, begins with the 'potamic' period, i.e., with the river culture of the Orient in Mesopotamia, of the Euphrates and the Tigris and the Nile, in the Assyrian, Babylonian, and Egyptian empires of the East. It is followed by the so-called thalassic period of a culture of inland seas and of the sea basin of the Mediterranean, to which Greek and Roman antiquity and the medieval Mediterranean belong. With the discovery of America and the circumnavigation of the earth the last and highest stage begins, the level of oceanic culture is attained."[95] It is only in the last, oceanic stage that a "spatial revolution," in Schmitt's understanding, came to pass.[96]

At the center of *Land and Sea* stands the question of spatial revolution. "A spatial revolution," Schmitt asks, "what is this?"[97] For Schmitt, something approximating a spatial revolution can occur without an elementary transformation—shifts of human engagement from the earth to the water or from the water to the air. In Schmitt's view, something approximating such a transformation accompanied "the first century of the Roman

93. Schmitt, *Land and Sea*, section 4, pp. 20–21, below. Cf. Ernst Kapp, *Philosophische oder Vergleichende Allgemeine Erdkunde als Wissenschaftliche Darstellung der Erdverhältnisse und des Menschenlebens nach ihrem inneren Zusammenhang* (*Philosophic or Comparative General Earth Science as [a] Scientific Representation of the Relations of the Earth and Human Life according their Inner Connectedness*), 2 vols. (Braunschweig: Verlag von Georg Westermann, 1845). In section four of *Land and Sea*, Schmitt refers to Kapp's work by its abbreviated title: *Vergleichende Allgemeine Erdkunde* (*Comparative General Earth Science*).
94. Cf. van Laak, "Von Alfred T. Mahan zu Carl Schmitt," p. 267 and 267n23.
95. Schmitt, *Land and Sea*, section 4, below.
96. van Laak, "Von Alfred T. Mahan zu Carl Schmitt," p. 275.
97. Schmitt, *Land and Sea*, section 10, p. 47, below.

imperial period"—in the century of Caesar, Augustus, Tiberius, Nero, Seneca, Paul, and the founders of Christianity. Schmitt writes that "In the first century of the Roman imperial period, most strongly indeed at the time of Nero, the consciousness of a deep transformation became so powerful and expansive that one can almost speak of spatial revolutionary transformations, at least with the leading intellects.... The field of vision expanded to the East and to the West, to the North and to the South. Wars of conquest and civil wars enveloped space from Spain to Persia, from England to Egypt. Widely distant regions and peoples came into contact with each other and experienced the unity of a common political destiny."[98]

However, for Schmitt, the first full spatial revolution begins with European exploration and conquest of the Americas, and with the altered conceptions of space that both generate and further these discoveries. Changes in spatial concepts are, in Schmitt's view, at the root of spatial revolutions. "There is more to a spatial revolution than landing in a heretofore unknown place," Schmitt writes. "A spatial revolution involves a change in the concepts of space encompassing all the levels and domains of human existence."[99] Art and architecture, Schmitt claims, are indexes of spatial revolutions, offering plastic and visible instances of altered spatial concepts and consciousness. "The painting of the Renaissance," Schmitt writes, "laid aside the space of medieval Gothic painting; the painters now painted humans and things placed in a space, which perspectivally generates an empty depth. Humans and things now stand and move *within* a space. In comparison with the space of a Gothic image, this signifies, in fact, another world."[100]

---

98. Ibid., section 11, pp. 50–51, below.
99. Ibid., section 12, p. 57, below.
100. Ibid., section 12, p. 58, below.

For Schmitt, it is spatial transformations that occasion elemental transformations. In a certain sense, for Schmitt, there is a dialectical relation between space and the elements. While elemental transformations are occasioned by spatial revolutions, it is only through the elements that peoples have an experience of space. The spatial revolution that both occasioned and accompanied the European conquests and discoveries in the sixteenth and seventeenth centuries, in Schmitt's theory, offers the occasion for an elemental transformation. This transformation, for Schmitt, is a turn from a terrestrial to a maritime existence, that is simultaneously the step between the second and third stages in Kapp's (and Schmitt's) triadic developmental picture—a shift between thalassic and oceanic existence, which marks a turn away from the land toward an existence based upon the expansive oceans.

While, for Schmitt, "World history is a history of land-appropriations [*Landnahmen*],"[101] the English effect a spatial revolution by appropriating the seas and the oceans of the world. "England is an island," Schmitt writes in *Land and Sea*. "However, only by first becoming the bearer and center of the elementary turn from the fixed land to the high sea, and only as the heiress of all the maritime energies released at that time, did it transform itself into the island, which is what one means when one ever and again intones that England is an island. And only in first becoming an island in a new, heretofore unknown sense did it complete the British maritime appropriation of the world oceans and complete the first phase of the planetary spatial revolution."[102] In Schmitt's opinion, this appropriation

101. Ibid., section 13, p. 63, below.
102. Ibid., section 17, below. Cf. Schmitt, *Dialogue on New Space* (1955/1958), section 3:"[Altmann:] Up until the sixteenth century, the island England was no more than a severed-off piece of the European continent, with its countenance turned toward the fixed land. Still in the fifteenth century, the English knights in France took a good haul of booty, as did the knights

of the seas forms the basis of nothing less than the industrial revolution.[103] The industrial revolution "had set in with the invention of machines in England in the eighteenth century. The first coal furnace (1735), the first cast-iron steel (1740), the steam engine (1768), the spinning jenny (1770), the mechanical loom (1786), all first in England, are several examples of England's great industrial advantage over all other peoples.[104] The steamship and the iron rail followed in the nineteenth century. Here, too, England remained in the lead. The great sea power simultaneously became the great machine power."[105] In Schmitt's presentation in *Land and Sea*, the English shift to a maritime existence effected a spatial revolution with the

---

of other lands as well. Just think about the age of the Virgin of Orléans! Up until the sixteenth century, the English were a people of shepherds who sold their wool to Flanders, where it was worked into cloth. And this people of shepherds metamorphosed in the sixteenth and seventeenth centuries into a people of sea-dogs. Now the island turns its countenance away from the continent and glances out upon the great seas of the world. It lifts anchor and becomes the bearer of power over an oceanic world empire." Schmitt, *Dialogues on Power and Space*, pp. 68–69.

103. Schmitt, *Land and Sea*, sections 17–18, below. Cf. Schmitt, *Dialogue on New Space* (1955/1958), section 4: "[Altmann:] The English took the ocean; the Russians took from Moscow out to Siberia and completed a purely terrestrial expansion. But how remarkable: on the basis of this gigantic Russian land appropriation, no industrial revolution emerged. The industrial revolution emerged on the island England, an island, the historical situation of which became incomparable because it had taken the step toward maritime existence." Schmitt, *Dialogues on Power and Space*, p. 71.

104. This passage is partially recapitulated in Schmitt's 1955 radio play *Dialogue on New Space* (*Gespräch über den Neuen Raum*), in Schmitt, *Staat, Großraum, Nomos*, p. 560: "N[eumeyer]. We all know where the industrial revolution comes from. The industrial revolution comes from England in the eighteenth century. The dates are to be found in all school textbooks: the first coal furnace in 1735; the first cast-iron steel in 1740; the first steam-engine in 1768; the first modern factory in Nottingham in 1769; the first spinning jenny in 1770; the mechanical loom in 1786, and so on up to the first steam locomotive in 1825."

105. Schmitt, *Land and Sea*, section 18, p. 84, below.

English appropriation of the seas. This sea appropriation, in turn, both formed the basis of English maritime hegemony and unleashed, in Schmitt's view, the energies that gave rise to the industrial revolution.

In his propaganda articles for *Das Reich* in 1940 and 1941, as well as in an article for the edited volume *Das Reich und Europa*,[106] Schmitt expressed the hope that a new spatial revolution was underway. The German *Reich* was expanding the sphere of its dominion, and Schmitt articulated the public hope that National Socialism might establish both land and air supremacy in continental Europe.[107] Writing in *Das Reich* in March 1941, Schmitt hopefully asserted that "The sea is no longer an element, but has rather become a space [*Raum*], as the air has also become a space of human activity and the exercise of human dominion. The contemporary spatial revolution is greater and deeper than that of the sixteenth and seventeenth centuries."[108] In his book chapter for *Das Reich und Europa*, originally delivered as a conference paper at Nuremberg in February 1941, Schmitt went even further, claiming that "the conquest of air space creates a new image of the world [*Weltbild*], which overcomes the prior separation of the elements of land and sea and puts through new spatial concepts, new measures and dimensions and with these also new spatial orders."[109]

106. Carl Schmitt, "Staatliche Souveränität und freies Meer: Über den Gegensatz von Land und See im Völkerrecht der Neuzeit," pp. 79–105, in *Das Reich und Europa* (Leipzig: Koehler & Amelang, 1941), reprinted in *Staat, Großraum, Nomos*, pp. 401–30; cf. Volpi, "Il potere degli elementi," p. 147; van Laak, "Von Alfred T. Mahan zu Carl Schmitt," p. 276n47.

107. Schmitt, "Staatliche Souveränität und freies Meer," pp. 416, 422; Schmitt, "Das Meer gegen das Land," pp. 1–2, in *Staat, Großraum, Nomos*, p. 398.

108. Schmitt, "Das Meer gegen das Land," pp. 1–2, in *Staat, Großraum, Nomos*, p. 398.

109. Schmitt, "Staatliche Souveränität und freies Meer," p. 422.

A new spatial revolution, Schmitt seemed to hope in February and March 1941, might consist in a revolution reorienting geopolitics toward *Großraum* spatial orders as well as toward a spatial order in which Germany might surpass British sea power with the aerial supremacy of the Luftwaffe—a spatial revolution from the element of water to the element of air.

However, with persistent Allied bombing of Germany throughout the summer of 1941 into 1942 along with the protracted battle with the Soviet Union, Schmitt's picture of aerial power changes between his February–March 1941 articles and *Land and Sea*.[110] *Land and Sea* ends not with a spatial revolution from the element of water to the element of air or with the victory of the Luftwaffe.[111] Rather, *Land and Sea* ends with a spatial revolution into the element of fire. As the book ends, the aerial bombardment of Nazi Germany picks up in earnest and the human enters the element of fire. In the element of fire, the world goes up in flames. With the spatial revolution from the element of air to the element of fire, a literary turn with perhaps more than a hint of the apocalyptic,[112] Schmitt gives his reader to understand that the war has already been lost.

---

110. For treatments of Schmitt on air power, see van Laak, "Von Alfred T. Mahan zu Carl Schmitt," p. 280; Armitage, "The Elephant and the Whale," p. 32; Nasser Hussain, "Air Power," in Stephen Legg, ed., *Spatiality, Sovereignty and Carl Schmitt*, pp. 244–50.

111. Cf. Schmitt's letter to Ernst Jünger, dated July 4, 1941: "By the way, the air has not somehow manifested itself as a new element through the Luftwaffe and the airplanes; the element related to the Luftwaffe is not the air, but rather the fire." ("Die Luft ist übrigens nicht etwa durch die Luftwaffe und Flugzeuge als neues Element erschienen; das der Luftwaffe zugeordnete Element ist nicht die Luft sondern das Feuer.") Jünger–Schmitt, *Briefe 1930–1983*, p. 121.

112. Taubes, *Ad Carl Schmitt*, section 1. Cf. Schmitt's letter to Ernst Jünger, dated December 10, 1942. Jünger–Schmitt, *Briefe 1930–1983*, p. 151.

## Conclusion

Whatever else it was or is or may be, Schmitt's *Land and Sea* was both written as a work of German National Socialist propaganda and also conceived as a critique of certain strands of Hitlerian geopolitics. As critique, however, it is not the kind of critique that an anti-Nazi might have hoped for or expected: it is a critique of Hitler for breaking his alliance with Stalin and Soviet Russia; it is a critique of those Hitlerian policies that, in Schmitt's view, did not tend toward the military and geopolitical advancement of Nazism. The same observer who portrayed *Land and Sea* as Schmitt's "most beautiful book"[113] would later claim that "The error of the Schmittian *oeuvre* is the truth of German history."[114] In the trappings of world history, in the motley company of Leviathans and Behemoths, pirates and poets, whale hunters and corsairs, Nazi ethnography and anti-Jewish polemic, these errors present themselves extravagantly and hauntingly in Carl Schmitt's *Land and Sea*.

---

113. Sombart, *Jugend in Berlin*, pp. 21, 255.
114. Sombart, *Die deutschen Männer und ihre Feinde*, p. 13: "Der Irrtum des Schmittschen Werkes ist die Wahrheit der deutschen Geschichte."

# Land and Sea
## A World-Historical Meditation[1]

1. Schmitt's subtitle, *Eine weltgeschichtliche Betrachtung, A World-Historical Meditation*, may contain a reference to Jacob Burckhardt's *Weltgeschichtliche Betrachtungen, World-Historical Meditations*, three copies of which (two German editions and an English translation) were held in Schmitt's postwar library: "Burckhardt, Jakob: Weltgeschichtliche Betrachtungen. Mit Nachw. hrsg. von Rudolf Marx (Kröners Taschenausgabe, 55), Leipzig [1928?] Semmel Nr. 103 Burckhardt, Jakob: Dass. [Hrsg. von Rudolf

Stadelmann], Tübingen 1949 Semmel Nr. 104 Burckhardt, Jakob: Reflections on history [Follows the text, with minor stylistic and spelling changes, of the transl. by 'M. D. H.' M. D. Hottinger. Introd. by Gottfried Dietze], Indianapolis 1979 (Mit Widmung) LAV NRW RW 265 Nr. 27758." Martin Tielke, "Die Bibliothek Carl Schmitts," Carl Schmitt Gesellschaft, Stand: 1.6.2015, pp. 63–64. Schmitt refers to Burckhardt's *Weltgeschichtliche Betrachtungen* in a letter to Ernst Jünger dated August 10, 1931. Cf. Ernst Jünger–Carl Schmitt, *Briefe 1930–1983*, 2nd ed., ed. Helmuth Kiesel (Stuttgart: Klett-Cotta, 2012 [1999]), p. 12. Schmitt also refers to Burckhardt's book in his postwar *Dialogue on Power and Access to the Holder of Power*. Cf. Carl Schmitt, *Dialogues on Power and Space*, ed. Federico Finchelstein and Andreas Kalyvas, trans. Samuel Garrett Zeitlin (Cambridge: Polity Press, 2015), pp. 41ff. Schmitt's German original contains one footnote in the 1942 edition and two footnotes in the 1954 and 1981 editions, each of which is marked as such. All other notes are those of the translator.

*Narrated to my daughter Anima*[2]

2. Anima Louise Schmitt, from 1957 onward Anima Schmitt de Otero (1931–83), Carl Schmitt's daughter and only child. Anima Schmitt de Otero was later the translator of Schmitt's *Ex Captivitate Salus, Dialogues, Theory of the Partisan,* and *The Tyranny of Values* from German into Spanish as well as translator of Lilian Winstanley's *Hamlet and the Scottish Succession* from English into German as *Hamlet, Sohn der Maria Stuart* (Pfullingen: Günther Neske Verlag, 1952), a volume for which Carl Schmitt wrote the preface. In

a letter to the jurist Rudolf Smend dated January 14, 1943, in which Schmitt enclosed a copy of *Land and Sea* for Smend as a birthday present, Schmitt writes: "As I here send you a poor little Reclam pamphlet and make it the bearer of my birthday greetings, you must understand and pardon it as emerging from the general leanness of the current situation. I would gladly have sent you something more beautiful and, at the very least, a hardback copy on better paper. But the publisher has refused all this as "forbidden" ["*verboten*"].... As the little book bears the dedication 'Narrated to my daughter Anima,' I did not intend to lay claim to any epic faculties and somehow to raise a comparison with Dickens's *A Child's History of England*; on the contrary, with this [dedication] I wish to secure the expectation of your leniency and clemency, without which I would not dare to appear before you with such a little thing." Carl Schmitt-Rudolf Smend, *"Auf der gefahrenvollen Straße des öffentlichen Rechts": Briefwechsel Carl Schmitt-Rudolf Smend 1921–1961: Mit ergänzenden Materialien*, 2nd rev. ed., ed. Reinhard Mehring (Berlin: Duncker & Humblot, 2012 [2010]), pp. 110–11.

**1**

The human is a land-being, a land-dweller.[3] He stands and walks and moves upon the firmly grounded earth. This is his standpoint and his soil; through it he receives his viewpoint; this

---

3. The first words of *Land and Sea*, in all the German editions, are "Der Mensch." It is not clear, for a variety of reasons, that Schmitt understands his notion of "the human" (*der Mensch*) to cover all that a contemporary reader might understand to be pertinent to the species *homo sapiens*. For reasons of philological and historical accuracy, in order to allow English readers to interpret Schmitt's notion of "the human" and to make both his political vocabulary as well as his political anthropology accessible to an English readership, *der Mensch* and its equivalents have been rendered as "the human" or "human" throughout. The alternative translation of *der Mensch* as "Man," adopted in the illegal translation of *Land und Meer* published by Plutarch Press in 1997, is infelicitous for several reasons. The translation of "Mensch" as "man" obscures Schmitt's engagements with National Socialism and National Socialist political vocabulary. National Socialist political vocabulary and propaganda distinguished *Untermenschen* from *Menschen* and *Menschen* from *Übermenschen*. Importantly, for National Socialism and for Schmitt not all human beings (members of the species *homo sapiens*) were *Menschen*—"Aryan" women could be *Menschen* but Jewish people in Nazi ideology—both men and women—do not qualify for the status of *Menschen*, as Schmitt makes particularly clear in *Land und Meer*, which he published in 1942, where landedness confers humanity (a claim repeated in the prologue to Schmitt's 1955 *Dialogue on New Space*) and the Jewish people lack a land (Schmitt claims that Jewish people are landless wanderers who live in tents in section 3 of the 1942 edition of *Land und Meer*) and thereby fail to qualify as human for Schmitt. Schmitt republished an edited version of *Land und Meer* in 1954, in the very year in which he went to work on *The Dialogue on Power*, in which he played down, but nonetheless preserved, this distinction. Both Adam and Eve are "Menschen," according to Schmitt in the immediate post–World War II period (*Ex Capitivate Salus* [1950], penultimate section, p. 79, "Wisdom of the Cell" [*Weisheit der Zelle*]), while the Jewish people, for Schmitt, do not qualify for this status. Cf. Samuel Garrett Zeitlin, "Translator's Introduction," in Schmitt, *Dialogues on Power and Space*, pp. vi–vii.

defines his impressions and his way of seeing the world. He receives not only his field of vision but also the form of his gait and his movements, his shape as a living being born and moving upon the earth. He consequently calls the planet on which he lives the "earth," although, with respect to the extent of its surface, it is known to be almost three quarters water and only one quarter earth, and, indeed, the largest pieces of earth within it only swim like islands. Since the time when we knew that this earth of ours had the shape of a sphere, we have spoken with the greatest self-evidence of this "ball of earth" and of this "terrestrial orb." You would find it strange if you had to imagine for yourself a "ball of sea" or a "maritime orb."

Our this-worldly being, happiness and unhappiness, joy and suffering, is for us the "earthly" life and—accordingly—an earthly paradise or an earthly vale of tears. Thus, it is understandable that in many myths and legends, in which peoples [*die Völker*] have stored up their oldest and deepest remembrances and experiences, the earth appears as the great mother of humans. She is marked as the oldest of all deities. Holy books tell us that the human comes from the earth and shall become earth again.[4] The earth is his motherly ground, he himself is accordingly a son of the earth. In his fellow humans he sees earthly brothers and citizens of the earth. Among the four traditional elements—earth, water, fire, and air—the earth is the element that is prescribed for humans and that most strongly defines the human. The thought that the human being could be shaped as strongly through another of the four elements as through the earth, appears at first glance as a merely phantasmic possibility. The human is no fish and no bird and, indeed, no fire-animal, should any such thing exist.

Are, consequently, human being and human essence in their core purely earthly and only directed toward the earth,

4. Cf. Genesis 3:17–18; Ecclesiastes 12:7.

and are the other elements really additive accretions to the earth, things of second rank? It's not so simple. The question, whether there is yet another mode of human existence different from that which is purely earth-defined, lies nearer than we think. You need only walk to the seashore and raise a glance and already the overwhelming surface of the sea encompasses your horizon. It is remarkable that the human, when he stands upon a shore, naturally gazes out from the land to the sea and not, conversely, from the sea to the land. In deep, often unconscious human memories, water and sea are the secret originary ground of all life. Most peoples [*Völker*] recall in their myths and legends not only earth-born gods and humans but also gods and humans sprung from the sea. Aphrodite, the goddess of feminine beauty, arose up out of the foam of the waves of the sea. The sea has brought forth other children as well, and we shall later become acquainted with "children of the sea"[5] and wild "sea dogs," who bear little resemblance to this enchanting image of foam-born feminine beauty. Suddenly, you see here a world other than the earth and other than the firm land. Now you can understand why poets, natural philosophers, and natural scientists seek the beginning of all life in water and why Goethe sings in celebratory verses:

> All is out of water sprung,
> All shall through the water stay,
> Ocean, bless us with your eternal sway![6]

---

5. Cf. Hosea 11:10 in the Latin Vulgate: "post Dominum ambulabunt quasi leo rugiet quia ipse rugiet et formidabunt filii maris." Hosea 11:10 is rendered in the Douay-Rheims translation as follows: "They shall walk after the Lord, he shall roar as a lion: because he shall roar, and the children of the sea shall fear."

6. Part of a speech of the character "Thales" in act 2 of the second part of Goethe's *Faust* (1832). Thales' speech runs: "THALES. Heil! Heil! aufs neue!/ Wie ich mich blühend freue,/ Vom Schönen, Wahren durchdrungen.../ Alles ist aus dem Wasser entsprungen!!/ Alles wird durch das Wasser

Most frequently the Greek natural philosopher Thales of Miletus (from around 500 BC) is named as the originator of the doctrine that locates the origin of all existence in the water. But this conception is older and simultaneously younger than Thales. It is eternal. In the last century, the nineteenth century, it was, in particular, a German scholar in the grand style, Lorenz Oken,[7] who explained human life, like all life, as emerging from the sea. In the family trees as well that were constructed by the Darwinian natural scientists, fish and land animals are found next to and following one another in different sequences. Here, animals of the sea figure as human ancestors. The originary and early history of humanity appears to confirm this oceanic origin. Important researchers have discovered that besides "autochthonal," i.e., land-born peoples, there have also been "autothalassic," i.e., peoples purely defined by the sea, who have never been land-dwellers, and who wished to know nothing of firm land, other than that it formed the boundaries of their purely maritime existence. On the isles of the South Sea, in the Polynesian seafarers, Canaks and Sawoiori, one recognizes still the last remnants of such fish-humans [*Fischmenschen*]. Their whole being, their conceptual world and language were related to the sea. To them our conceptions of space and time attained from fixed land appeared as strange and incomprehensible as, conversely, the world of these pure sea-humans [*Seemenschen*] signifies a hardly comprehensible other world for us land-humans [*Landmenschen*].

Therefore, it is a persistent question: what is our element? Are we children of the land or of the sea? This question does

---

erhalten! / Ozean, gönn uns dein ewiges Walten. / Wenn du nicht Wolken sendetest, / Nicht reiche Bäche spendetest, / Hin und her nicht Flüsse wendetest, / Die Ströme nicht vollendetest, / Was wären Gebirge, was Ebnen und Welt? / Du bist's, der das frischeste Leben erhält."

7. Lorenz Oken (1779–1851) was a German naturalist and proponent of vitalism.

not allow itself to be answered with a simple either–or. Ancient myths, modern natural scientific hypotheses, and the results of research into early history leave both possibilities open.

2

The word "element" is, of all things, still[8] in need of a brief explanation. From the time of the previously mentioned philosopher Thales, since the Ionian natural philosophy of the pre-Socratic thinkers, thus, since roughly 500 years before the common era, the European peoples have spoken of the four elements. Since then, the four elements—earth, water, air, and fire—despite all scientific critique up to the present day, have remained an inextinguishably living notion. Modern natural science has dissolved the four elements; today, natural science distinguishes more than ninety, wholly otherwise structured "elements," and understands by this all basic material that cannot be disaggregated or dissolved with contemporary chemical methods. The elements, with which they work in the practical as in the theoretical domain, thus have with those four originary materials only the word in common. Today, no physicist or chemist would say that one of the four old elements is the only "basic material" of the world, as Thales of Miletus asserted of water, as Heraclitus of Ephesus asserted of fire, as Anaximenes of Miletus asserted of air, and as Empedocles of Agrigentum asserted of a combination of the four root-stems. Already, the question of what originary matter, basic matter, stem and root here actually mean would lead us into unforeseeable problems of natural scientific physics and equally unforeseeable problems of metaphysics and epistemology. Nonetheless, for our historical meditation, we can stick with the four elements. For us, these elements are precisely simple and descriptive names. They are

---

8. The word "still" (*noch*) is an addition of the 1954 edition that is preserved in the 1981 edition.

collective signifiers, which point to different grand possibilities of human existence. Therefore, we may still deploy them today and we may speak of land powers and sea powers in the sense of such elements.

Thus, the "elements" of land and sea, with which the following discourse is concerned, must not be conceived as mere natural scientific quantities. Otherwise, they would decompose themselves into chemical material, that is, into a historical nothing. The designations, which proceed from them, in particular the land-oriented or sea-oriented forms of historical existence, do not run their course in a mechanically compulsory way. If the human were nothing other than a living being completely defined by his environment, then the human would be, accordingly, a land animal, or a fish, or a bird, or a phantasmic mixture of these elementary designations. The pure types of the four elements, especially the pure earth-humans and the pure sea-humans, had little to do with one another; they would be opposed to one another without relation, and, indeed, the purer they would be, the less they would relate to one another. The mixtures would result in good or bad types and would cultivate friendships or enmities like chemical affinities or contrasts. The being and fate of the humans would be defined wholly naturally, like that of an animal or a plant. One could only say that certain ones devour the others, while others again live together in symbiosis. There would be no human history other than human deed and human resolve.

Now, however, the human is a being which is not completely taken up with its environment. The human has the strength to historically conquer his existence [*Dasein*] and consciousness. The human is aware not only of birth but also of the possibility of rebirth. In some distress and danger, in which the animal and the plant are helplessly destroyed, the human can save himself for a new existence through his spirit, through unerring observation, through drawing entailments, and through resolve. The human has some latitude for his power and his historical empowerment. The human is capable of choice, and in certain historical moments he can even choose the element in which he determines himself as a new collective form of his historical existence through his own deed and his own achievement and the element in which he organizes himself. In this sense, rightly understood, the human has, as the poet says, "the freedom to break out where he will."[9]

3

World history is a history of the battle of sea powers against land powers and of land powers against sea powers. A French specialist in military science, the Admiral Castex, gave his strategic book the comprehensive subtitle: *The Sea against the Land, la Mer contre la Terre*.[10] With this subtitle, he remains within a great tradition.

For ages, the elementary opposition between land and sea has been noted, and still near the end of the nineteenth century it was a beloved image to depict the tensions of the time between Russia and England as the battle of a bear with a whale-fish.[11] The whale-fish is the great, mythic fish, the Leviathan, of

---

9. This appears to be a reference to the last six words of Friedrich Hölderlin's poem "Lebenslauf" ("Curriculum vitae"), from 1800.

10. Schmitt seems here to refer to Admiral Raoul Castex (1878–1968) and his multi-volume *Théories stratégiques* (1929–35), which appeared in multiple editions. Volume five of the work, published in 1935, bears the subtitle *la mer contre la terre*. Cf. Carl Schmitt, *Staat, Großraum, Nomos*, ed. Günter Maschke (Berlin: Duncker & Humblot, 1995), p. 425n[14]. Schmitt's orthography, capitalizing the French nouns, has been retained in the translation above.

11. Schmitt deploys the terms "Walfisch" (whale-fish) and "Walfischjäger" (whale-fish hunter), already antiquated in German common usage in the 1940s (as well as the 1950s and 1980s), and he further asserts that whales are

which we shall have to hear something still, the bear one of many symbolic representatives of land animals.[12] According to medieval interpretations[13] of the so-called Kabbalists, world history is a battle between the powerful whale-fish, the Leviathan, and the equally strong land animal, the Behemoth, which is imagined as a bull or as an elephant.[14] Both names, Leviathan

---

fish, for reasons of his own that he elaborates below, in section 5 of *Land und Meer*. Schmitt's purposefully antiquated vocabulary is rendered with antiquated English equivalents.

12. Here, in the 1954 and 1981 (and subsequent) editions, Schmitt has omitted a sentence from his 1942 text: "The Jews have conceived for themselves the battle between land and sea in their own way." Schmitt (1942), p. 9: "Die Juden haben sich den Kampf zwischen Land und Meer auf ihre Weise zurechtgelegt." Cf. Schmitt (1954), p. 8. The 1942 version of the sentence is retained in the 1952 Spanish translation by Rafael Fernandez-Quintanilla. Carl Schmitt, *Tierra y Mar, Consideraciones sobre la historia universal*, trans. Rafael Fernandez-Quintanilla (Madrid: Instituto de Estudios Políticos [Series: Colección Civitas], 1952), p. 16.

13. Here, in the 1954 and 1981 (and subsequent) editions, Schmitt has omitted a descriptive clause from his 1942 text, "of Jewish secret doctrines." Schmitt (1942), p. 9: "Nach mittelalterlichen Deutungen *jüdischer Geheimlehren, nach den* sogenannten Kabbalisten, ist die Weltgeschichte ein Kampf zwischen dem mächtigen Walfisch, dem Leviathan, und dem ebenso starken Landtier, dem Behemoth, den man sich als einen Stier oder Elefanten vorstellte" (italics added for the clause removed and altered). Cf. Schmitt (1954), p. 8; Raphael Gross, *Carl Schmitt und die Juden: Eine deutsche Rechtslehre* (Frankfurt am Main: Suhrkamp, 2005 [2000]), pp. 274–77; Heinrich Meier, *Die Lehre Carl Schmitts: Vier Kapitel zur Unterscheidung Politischer Theologie und Politischer Philosophie* (Stuttgart-Weimar: J. B. Metzler, 2009 [1994]), pp. 237–40. The 1942 version of the sentence is retained in the 1952 Spanish translation by Fernandez-Quintanilla; see Schmitt, *Tierra y Mar* (1952), p. 16.

14. Schmitt may make reference here to the Babylonian Talmud, Tractate Baba Bathra, Folios 74a–75a. The translator is grateful to Professor Ron Hassner and to Raphael Magarik for this reference. Rafael Gross comments on this passage (and a parallel passage in the first chapter of Schmitt's 1938 book *Der Leviathan in der Staatslehre des Thomas Hobbes, Sinn und Fehlschlag eines politischen Symbols*) as follows: "It remains unclear which specific Kabbalistic texts, if any, Schmitt has in mind. A legend of God playing with Leviathan three hours a day is found in Rabbinic literature; and in one Talmudic tractate (Baba Bathra 74b) Rabbi Jochanan indicates that at some point

and Behemoth, stem from the Book of Job (chapters 40 and 41). Now, the Kabbalists say that the Behemoth exerts itself to rip apart the Leviathan with its horns or teeth, while the Leviathan, on the contrary, holds shut the mouth and nose of the land animal with its fins so that it cannot eat or breathe. This is, as descriptive as only a mythic image is capable of being, the sketch of the blockade of a land power by a sea power, which cuts off the land from supplies in order to starve it out. Thus[15] do both fighting powers mutually kill each other.[16] The Jews,

---

God will 'prepare a meal for the pious from the flesh of Leviathan.' But any reference here to a tie between the state or heathen peoples and Leviathan is absent. With Schmitt citing not the Talmud but unnamed Kabbalistic texts, the strong possibility emerges that he is referring to Kabbalistic knowledge metaphorically." Rafael Gross, *Carl Schmitt and the Jews: The "Jewish Question," the Holocaust, and German Legal Theory*, trans. Joel Golb (Madison: Univ. of Wisconsin Press, 2007), p. 158; Gross, *Carl Schmitt und die Juden*, p. 273 and 273n25; Meier, *Die Lehre Carl Schmitts*, pp. 237–40.

15. Here, in the 1954 and 1981 (and subsequent) editions, Schmitt has omitted a three-word clause from his 1942 text: "meinen diese Juden" ("these Jews claim"). Schmitt (1942), p. 10; cf. Schmitt (1954), p. 8. A rendering of the 1942 version of the sentence is retained in the 1952 Spanish translation by Fernandez-Quintanilla; see Schmitt, *Tierra y Mar* (1952), p. 17: "piensan tales rabínos."

16. This sentence and the next differ substantially between the 1942 edition, on the one hand, and the 1954 and 1981 (and subsequent) editions, on the other. In the 1942 edition, this sentence and the following sentence, reiterating what may amount to blood libel against the Jewish people, read as follows: "So töten sich, meinen diese Juden, die beiden kämpfenden Mächte gegenseitig. Die Juden aber, sagen sie weiter, stehen daneben und sehen dem Kampfe zu. Sie essen das Fleisch der sich gegenseitig tötenden Tiere, ziehen ihnen die Haut ab, bauen sich aus dem Fell schöne Zelte und feiern ein festliches, tausendjähriges Gastmahl. So deuten die Juden die Weltgeschichte." ("Thus, these Jews claim, both the fighting powers mutually kill one another. The Jews, however, they say further, stand back and behold the battle [as spectators]. They eat the flesh of the beasts who mutually kill each other, remove the skin, and from the hide build themselves fine tents and celebrate a festive, millennial feast. Thus do the Jews interpret world history.") Schmitt (1942), p. 10; Schmitt (1954), pp. 8–9; Gross, *Carl Schmitt und die Juden*, pp. 274–77; Meier, *Die Lehre Carl Schmitts*, pp. 237–40. In altering and removing this

however, these Kabbalists say further, then celebrate the festive millennial "Feast of the Leviathan," which Heinrich Heine narrated in a famous poem.[17] The Kabbalist who is most often cited

---

passage from the paragraph, Schmitt modifies the depiction of Jews in the original edition for the republication in 1954 and 1981. The 1942 version of these sentences is retained in the 1952 Spanish translation by Fernandez-Quintanilla; see Schmitt, *Tierra y Mar* (1952), p. 17: "Así interpretan los judíos la historia universal."

17. Schmitt's reference to Heinrich Heine (1797–1856) is not present in the 1942 edition, but it is present in the 1954 and 1981 editions. Schmitt (1942), p. 10; Schmitt (1954), pp. 8–9; Schmitt (1981), p. 17; Gross, *Carl Schmitt und die Juden*, pp. 274–77; Meier, *Die Lehre Carl Schmitts*, pp. 237–40. In referring to Heine, Schmitt appears to refer to the terminal poem "Disputation," from the third section, *Hebräische Melodien* (*Hebraic Melodies*), of Heine's 1851 collection *Romanzero, Gedichte*. According to the editor of the Schmitt–Jünger correspondence, Helmuth Kiesel, Ernst Jünger makes reference to this poem in a letter to Schmitt dated August 28, 1941. Jünger–Schmitt, *Briefe 1930–1983*, pp. 127, 564. Heine's "Disputation" versifies an argument between a Jewish rabbi (Juda) and a Franciscan monk (Frater José) before the medieval court of Toledo in Castile. In Heine's poem, the monk and the rabbi dispute the truth of Christianity and Judaism with each party aiming to convert and either baptize or circumcise the converted opponent. In Heine's "Disputation," Heine's rabbi "Juda" offers the taste of Leviathan, served in broth to the chosen on the day of resurrection, as an enticement for Frater José to convert to Judaism. The relevant passage of the poem (ll. 293–328), the whole of which is spoken by Heine's character, the rabbi Juda, might be translated as follows:

> Leviathan the fish is called
> Which houses at the sea's floor
> With him plays God the Lord
> Every day for an hour—
>
> Except on the ninth
> Day of the Month of Av, when
> Indeed His Temple was reduced into ash;
> On that day is He too grief-stricken.
>
> The length of the Leviathan
> Is a hundred miles long, it has fin-feathers
> Great like King Og of Bashan
> And its tail is like a cedar.

for this historical interpretation of the Feast of the Leviathan is Isaac Abravanel. He lived from 1437 until 1508, in the age of the great discoveries; he was treasurer first to the King of Portugal

> Nonetheless, its flesh is delicate,
> More delicate than turtle,
> And on the Day of Resurrection
> The Lord shall call to table
>
> All pious chosen ones,
> The just and the wise—
> The Lord Our God's favorite fish
> They shall feast upon,
>
> Partly with white garlic-broth,
> Partly brown boiled in wine,
> With spices and raisins,
> Something like matelote.
>
> In the white garlic broth,
> Swim little grated radishes—
> Thus prepared, Frater José,
> You'd mouth down the fish, I bet!
>
> The brown sauce too is so tasty,
> Namely the sauce of raisins,
> Well will it heavenly please
> Your tummy, Frater José.
>
> What God cooks is cooked well!
> Monk-y, now, heed my counsel,
> Offer up the old foreskin
> And sate yourself on Leviathan.

The passages that Schmitt removed from the 1942 edition and the passages that Schmitt retained in the 1954 and 1981 editions are missing in several respects from Heine's poem. First, Heine's "Disputation" makes no mention of Behemoth, and thus no mention of the battle between Behemoth and Leviathan, nor does he mention Jewish spectatorship of this battle. Second, Heine's "Disputation" makes no mention of the Jews skinning the Leviathan and using the hide of Leviathan to make tents, emphasized in Schmitt's 1942 edition. Third, in Heine's "Disputation" it is never mentioned who kills Leviathan, but, according to Heine's character Juda, it is God who offers the meat of the Leviathan to the chosen, the wise, and the just.

then to the King of Castile and died in 1508 as a great man in Venice.[18] Thus, he knew the world and its riches, and he knew what he said.

Now, let us cast a glance upon certain developments of the great history of the world from the point of view of this battle between land and sea.

The world of Greek antiquity emerged from the voyages and wars of sea-peoples. "Not in vain did the sea god raise them."[19] A sea power ruling on the island of Crete expelled the pirates from the eastern part of the Mediterranean and created a culture, the inexplicable charm of which has become visible to us through the excavations of Knossos. A millennium later the free city of Athens defended itself in the sea battle at Salamis (480 BC) against its enemy, the "far-ruling Persians,"[20] behind wooden walls, that is to say on ships, and through this sea battle saved itself. Their own power in the Peloponnesian War was inferior to the land power Sparta, which, however, as

---

18. On this passage, Heinrich Meier notes: "Schmitt does not mention that three times in his life Abravanel was compelled to emigrate and died separated from his family." Meier, *Die Lehre Carl Schmitts*, p. 238n89; cf. Gross, *Carl Schmitt und die Juden*, p. 276.

19. A quotation that appears to be a reference to Friedrich Hölderlin's poem "The Archipelago" ("Der Archipelagus"), first published in 1804. Schmitt has changed the singular object ("ihn") in Hölderlin's original to a plural ("sie"). In a letter dated July 24, 1934, Ernst Jünger writes to Schmitt discussing this poem. Jünger–Schmitt, *Briefe 1930–1983*, p. 38.

20. A quotation that appears to be a reference to Hölderlin's poem "The Archipelago" ("Der Archipelagus"). The quotation draws from the line following that of the previous footnote: "Lauschet und sitzt und nicht umsonst erzog ihn der Meergott. / Denn des Genius Feind, der vielgebietende Perse, / Jahrlang zählt' er sie schon, der Waffen Menge, der Knechte, / Spottend des griechischen Lands und seiner wenigen Inseln, / Und sie deuchten dem Herrscher ein Spiel und noch, wie ein Traum, war / Ihm das innige Volk, vom Göttergeiste gerüstet." As in the previous reference to Hölderlin, Schmitt has changed the singular ("der...Perse") in Hölderlin's original to a plural ("die...Perser").

a land power, was not in a condition to unite the Hellenic cities and tribes and to lead a Greek Empire [*Reich*]. Rome, on the contrary, which from its foundations was an Italian republic of peasant farmers and a pure land power, grew up to an empire in the battle with the sea and trade power Carthage. Roman history is often both as a whole and also in particular in this episode of the long struggle between Rome and Carthage, compared with other world-historical confrontations and situations. Such comparisons and parallels can be very instructive, but they can also often lead to remarkable contradictions. For example, the English world empire is sometimes placed in parallel with Carthage, but at other times in parallel with Rome. Comparisons of this kind are mostly a two-ended stick, which one can grab from either side and turn around.

Vandals, Saracens, Vikings, and Normans struck rule of the sea from the hand of the declining Roman Empire. After many setbacks, the Arabs conquered Carthage (698) and founded the new capital city of Tunis. With this began their centuries-long rule of the western Mediterranean. The East Roman Byzantine Empire, ruled from Constantinople outward, was a coastal empire [*Küstenreich*]. It still had a strong fleet at its disposal and possessed a secret weapon, the so-called Greek fire. Nonetheless, it was pressed wholly into defense. In any case, Byzantium sought to accomplish something as a sea power, which the empire of Charlemagne—a pure land power—did not; Byzantium was a true "forestaller,"[21] a "Katechon,"[22] as one calls it in Greek; it "held out," despite its weakness, for many centuries against Islam and thereby hindered the Arabs from conquering

---

21. Here Schmitt deploys the term "Aufhalter" to render "Katechon"—the same translation used by Martin Luther in his sixteenth-century German vernacular translation of the Bible. Cf. Gopal Balakrishnan, *The Enemy: An Intellectual Portrait of Carl Schmitt* (London: Verso, 2000), pp. 221–25; Meier, *Die Lehre Carl Schmitts*, pp. 243–49.

22. Cf. 2 Thessalonians 2:6–7.

all of Italy.[23] Otherwise, as it transpired at the time with North Africa under the extinction of the ancient Christian culture, Italy would have been incorporated into the Islamic world. Lifted up by the Crusades, a new sea power then emerged in the Christian-European domains: Venice.

With this, a new mythic name is called into the great history of the world. For almost half a millennium the republic of Venice was seen as the symbol of dominion of the sea and of wealth founded on sea trade, as the splendid achievement of high politics and simultaneously as "the most curious creation in all periods of economic history."[24] Everything that the England-swooners from the eighteenth to the twentieth centuries

---

23. In a letter to Ernst Forsthoff dated June 20, 1942, Schmitt writes: "In relation to the great question, what κατέχων in 2 Thess. 2, 6/7 means, I have also re-entered into a correspondence with President Horn in Duisburg." Ernst Forsthoff–Carl Schmitt, *Briefwechsel (1926–1974)*, ed. Dorothee Mußgnug, Reinhard Mußgnug, and Angela Reinthal (Berlin: Akademie Verlag, 2007), p. 46. For further discussion of Schmitt's notion of the "Katechon," see Carl Schmitt, *The Nomos of the Earth in the International Law of the Jus Publicum Europaeum*, trans. G. L. Ulmen (New York: Telos Press, 2006 [2003]), pp. 59–63, 87, 238. Schmitt writes: "In the Middle Ages, Christian princes and peoples of Europe considered Rome or Jerusalem to be the center of the earth and regarded themselves as part of the Old World. Many thought that the world was old and close to ruin. For example, this attitude dominates part of Otto Freising's historical work. It was consistent with the Christian concept of the world, which saw the empire as a restrainer (*katechon*) of the Antichrist." Ibid., p. 87.

24. While the direct source for this unmarked quotation could not be determined, and it remains an unattributed quotation in all the German editions as well as in the French, Italian, and Spanish translations of *Land und Meer*, the thought present in the quotation may merit comparison with the section on Venice (*Venedig*) in Ernst Kapp, *Philosophische oder Vergleichende Allgemeine Erdkunde als Wissenschaftliche Darstellung der Erdverhältnisse und des Menschenlebens nach ihrem inneren Zusammenhang* (*Philosophic or Comparative General Earth Science as [a] Scientific Representation of the Relations of the Earth and Human Life according their Inner Connectedness*) (Braunschweig: Verlag von Georg Westermann, 1845), vol. 2, pp. 9–10, where Kapp treats both the economic situation of Venice and putative claims to the

have admired in England was already previously admired in Venice: the great wealth; the diplomatic superiority, with which the sea power knew how to exploit the oppositions between the land powers and to conduct its wars through others; the aristocratic constitution, which appeared to have solved the problem of internal political order; the toleration with respect to religious and philosophical opinions; the asylum for liberal ideas and for political emigration. To this, there is added the enchanting charm of splendid festivals and artistic beauty. One of these festivals has particularly occupied the human imagination and helped to bear the fame of Venice, the myth-shrouded "marriage with the sea," the so-called *sposalizio del mare*.[25] Annually on the day before[26] Christ's Ascension Day, the day of the "Sensa" (i.e., Ascensione),[27] the Doge of the Republic of Venice sailed upon the ship of pomp and state, the *Bucentoro*, out into the sea and threw a ring into the tides as a sign of the bond with the sea. The Venetians themselves, their neighbors, and peoples from far off saw in this a persuasive symbol, which gave a mythic consecration to sea-born power and sea-born wealth. But we shall yet see how things truly stood with this beautiful symbol when we approach it anew from a more elementary perspective.

This fabled queen of the sea shone in growing splendor from the year 1000 up to the year 1500. Around 1000, Nikephoros Phokas, then the Byzantine Emperor, could still

---

divine origin of Venetian architecture. Schmitt explicitly mentions both Kapp and this text in the following section, section 4, of *Land and Sea*.

25. The phrase "sposalizio del mare" is in Italian in Schmitt's original German. Schmitt (1942), p. 12; Schmitt (1954), p. 11; Schmitt (1981), p. 20.

26. Schmitt's text reads "before" ("vor") in the 1942, 1954, and 1981 editions. In twenty-first-century Venice, the "marriage with the sea" is celebrated on Ascension Day itself.

27. "Sensa" and "Ascensione" are, respectively, Venetian dialect and Italian in Schmitt's original text. "Sensa" is the Venetian dialect equivalent of "ascension."

claim of himself with some justification: "The dominion over the sea lies with me alone." Five-hundred years later, the Turkish Sultan in Constantinople explained to the Venetians, "Until now you were married to the sea, from now on it belongs to me." Between these two dates lies the period of Venetian sea power over the Adriatic, the Aegean Sea, and the eastern part of the Mediterranean. In this period there arose a legend, which still in the nineteenth and twentieth centuries drew numerous travelers and famous romantics from all European nations—poets and artists like Byron, Musset, Richard Wagner, Barrès—to Venice. No one can evade the magic of this legend, and nothing lies farther from us than to darken the glow of such splendor. If, however, we pose the question whether here lies before us a case of pure maritime existence and of real decision for the element of the sea, then we see immediately how confined a sea power restricted to the Adriatic and the Mediterranean basin is, once the unsurveyable spaces of the world oceans open themselves.

4

A German philosopher of geography whose spirit still bore the comprehensive thought-world of Hegel, Ernst Kapp, defined in a "Comparative General Earth Science" (1845)[28] the material stages of the empires of the water. He distinguishes three stages of development, three acts of a great drama. World history, for him, begins with the "potamic" period, i.e., with the river culture of the Orient in Mesopotamia, of the Euphrates and the Tigris and the Nile, in the Assyrian, Babylonian, and Egyptian empires of the East. It is followed by the so-called thalassic period of a culture of inland seas and of the sea basin of the Mediterranean, to which Greek and Roman antiquity and the

28. Schmitt here seems to refer to Kapp's *Philosophische oder Vergleichende Allgemeine Erdkunde*. Schmitt refers to Kapp's work by its abbreviated title: *Vergleichende Allgemeine Erdkunde* (*Comparative General Earth Science*).

medieval Mediterranean belong.[29] With the discovery of America and the circumnavigation of the earth the last and highest stage begins, the level of oceanic culture is attained, the bearers of which are Germanic peoples. To become clearer about the state of things, we would like, just once, to deploy this tripartite schema, which distinguishes river, inland sea, and ocean. We shall then see more clearly what it means that the sea power of Venice remained wholly on the second, thalassic level.

Precisely a festival such as the previously mentioned "Marriage with the Sea" discloses this distinction. Such actions symbolic of a bond with the sea are also present with other peoples who depend on the sea. For example, Indian tribes of Central America, who practice fishery and sea travel, have sacrificed rings and other treasures, animals, and even humans to the deities of the sea. However, I do not believe that Vikings and authentic "sea dogs" performed such ceremonies. They need not, on this account, be deemed less pious, and, perhaps, they had no less of an impulse to summon divine forces. However, they did not think of the ceremony of an engagement or marriage with the sea, precisely because they were real children of the sea.[30] They felt themselves identical with the element of the sea. This symbolic engagement or marriage, on the contrary, presupposes that the sacrificing party and the deity, to whom he sacrifices, are distinct, indeed, even opposed essences. Through such sacrifices a foreign element was to be placated. In the case of Venice, the ceremony allows for the distinct recognition that the symbolic act does not receive its sense from an elementary maritime existence; here, rather, a highly developed coastal and lagoon culture created for itself its own particular style of festive symbols. Mere navigation of the sea and a culture erected

---

29. In the 1981 text, the terminal verb is changed from a singular "gehört" (1942, p. 14; 1954, p. 12) to a plural "gehören" (1981).

30. Cf. Hosea 11:10 in the Latin Vulgate.

upon the exploitation of an advantageous coastal position is indeed something other than resituating a complete historical existence from the land to the sea as into another element.

The coastal empire of Venice begins around the year 1000 with a "flotilla promenade" to Dalmatia. Venice's rule over the hinterland, e.g., over Croatia or Hungary, always remained as problematic as only the rule of a flotilla over a country can be. From a naval technological perspective as well, up until its fall in the year 1797, the Republic of Venice never left the Mediterranean and the medieval period. Like the peoples of the Mediterranean, Venice knew only the oared vessel, the galley. The great sailed seafaring vessel, on the contrary, came from the Atlantic Ocean into the Mediterranean. The Venetian fleet was and remained a fleet of great galleys, propelled by the force of oars. The sail, as it was already in antiquity, was a supplement unfurled for auspicious rearward winds. A particular nautical achievement was the perfection of the compass into its modern form. Through the compass "something spiritual was breathed into the ship, as a result of which the human enters into community and a relationship with the vessel" (Kapp).[31] Now, for

31. Schmitt here appears to quote from the first volume of Kapp's *Philosophische oder Vergleichende Allgemeine Erdkunde*, pp. 261–62. The passage from which the quotation is drawn runs as follows: "Seitdem der Steuermann nicht mehr bloß die Hand am Steuer hat, sondern auch zugleich das Auge auf den Compaß richtet, seitdem dieser ein integrierender Theil des Schiffskörpers geworden ist, ist gleichsam etwas Geisthaftes dem Schiffe eingehaucht worden, vermöge dessen der Mensch mit dem Fahrzeug eine Gemeinschaft und Verwandtschaft eingeht, welche ihm dasselbe so vollständig in seine Macht gegeben haben, daß die entferntesten Gelände aller Oceane miteinander in Berührung treten—et ingens pateat tellus!" This passage might be rendered as follows: "Since the pilot no longer merely has his hand on the rudder, but rather also simultaneously has his eye on the compass, since this has become an integral part of the body of the ship, at the same time something spiritual was inspired in the ship, as a result of which the human enters into community and a relationship with the vessel, which has so fully given him its power that the farthest lands of all the oceans come into contact

the first time, the most distant terrains of all the oceans come into contact with one another, so that the globe expands. However, the modern compass, the appearance of which is usually set in the Italian coastal city of Amalfi in the year 1302, in any case did not originate in Venice. A deployment of this new means for oceanic voyages lay far from the Venetians.

We do not wish to diminish, as I have already said and yet again repeat, the splendor and fame of Venice. But we must make clear what it means for a people in its entire historical existence to decide for the sea as another element. The ways and means of fighting sea battles at that time show best what is at stake here and how little an elementary resituating of the entirety of human existence from the land onto the sea can be spoken of in the Mediterranean of that time. In the ancient style of sea battle, the oar-hauled ships pushed up against one another and attempted to ram and to board each other. In this way, sea battle is always battle at close quarters. "Like pairs of wrestling men, the ships grapple with each other."[32] The Romans first boarded enemy ships in the Battle of Mylae,[33] by throwing across boards

---

with one another—*et ingens pateat tellus* [and the mighty earth opens / alt: the world opens up to the ingenious (person)]!" The final Latin tag in the Kapp passage here cited by Schmitt itself appears to be a quotation from Seneca's *Medea*, ll. 373–79, in a passage spoken by the Chorus of Corinthians (*Chorus Corinthiorum*) and which Schmitt will partially quote (omitting the line that concludes the Kapp paragraph) in section 11 of *Land and Sea*: "Indus gelidum potat Araxen, / Albin Persae Rhenumque bibunt. / venient annis saecula seris, / quibus Oceanus vincula rerum / laxet et ingens pateat tellus / Tethysque novos detegat orbes, / nec sit terris ultima Thule." Seneca, *Medea*, ll. 373–79, in *L. Annaei Senecae Tragoediae*, rec. Rudolfus Peiper et Gustavus Richter (Bibliotheca scriptorum Graecorum et Romanorum Teubneriana) (Lipsiae, 1937), pp. 131–32. Cf. section 11 of *Land and Sea* below. The translator is thankful to Lars Vinx for help with this reference.

32. An apparent reference to and quotation from Hölderlin's poem "Der Archipelagus."

33. The Battle of Mylae (260 BCE) was a naval battle in the First Punic War between Carthage and Rome.

and in such a way set up a bridge, upon which they could enter the enemy ship. Sea battle thereby became land battle aboard ships. One fought with swords upon the shipboards as upon a stage. The great sea battles of antiquity were played out in this way. According to the same principle, even if with more primitive hand weapons, Malay and Indian tribes conducted their sea battles with each other.

The last great sea battle of this kind was simultaneously the last famous deed of Venetian history: the Sea Battle of Lepanto (1571). Here, the Spanish-Venetian fleet collided together with the Turkish fleet and achieved the greatest sea victory that Christians have borne away from Mohammedans.[34] The battle took place in the same location in which, shortly before the beginning of the common era, the fleets of the East and of the West, of Antony and of Octavian, collided at Actium (30 BC). The Sea Battle of Lepanto was still fought with essentially the same means of naval technology with which the Battle of Actium had been fought a millennium and a half earlier. Elite Spanish foot soldiers, the famed Tercios, attacked the Janissaries, the elite troops of the Ottoman Empire, in a battle at close quarters fought upon the shipboards.

Only a few years after Lepanto, the transformation of the conduct of naval warfare occurred with the defeat of the Spanish Armada (1588) in the channel between England and the Continent. The small sailing ships of the English proved themselves superior to the great Spanish ships of state. It was however not the English, but rather the Dutch, who were at that time the leaders in the domain of shipbuilding technology. In the period from 1450 to 1600, the Dutch invented more new ship types than all the other peoples. The mere discovery of new parts of the earth and new oceans would not have sufficed

---

34. "Mohammedans," here, renders Schmitt's "Mohammedaner." Schmitt (1942), p. 17; Schmitt (1954), p. 14; Schmitt (1981), p. 27.

to establish rule over the world's seas and a decision for the sea as an element.

## 5

Not noble Doges on pomp-laden ships of state, but rather wild adventurers and sea dogs, clever ocean-strafing whale hunters and daring sailors are the first heroes of a new maritime existence. In two essential domains, in whale hunting and in shipbuilding, the Dutch, at the outset, were far superior.

Here, I must first say a word in praise of the whale and in honor of the whale hunters. It is not possible to speak of the great history of the sea, and of the human decision for the element of the sea, without commemorating the fabled Leviathan and its equally fabled hunter. This is, admittedly, an enormous theme. My weak praise measures up neither to the whale nor to the whale-fish hunter. How can I dare tell, in an adequate way, of two wonders of the sea, of the most powerful of all living beasts and of the most cunning of human hunters?

I can only dare it because I am an adherent of two great heralds and messengers of both of these wonders of the sea, of an eloquent French historian, Jules Michelet, and a great American poet, Herman Melville. The Frenchman published a book on the sea in the year 1861, a hymn to the beauty of the sea and the world of its undiscovered wonders,[35] to the richness of whole continents, which receive their life and growth from the sea floor and which the "cruel King of this world,"[36] the human,

---

35. Here and throughout, "[das] Wunder" and "[die] Wunder" (pl.) are translated as "wonder" and "wonders," respectively, but might also be translated as "miracle" or "miracles."

36. Here, Schmitt appears to refer to a passage from Jules Michelet's 1861 text *La mer* (*The Sea*), in which Michelet writes: "La mer commença tout, sans doute. Mais ce n'est pas de plus haut animaux de mer que sortit la série parallèle des formes terrestres dont l'homme est le couronnement. Ils étaient trop fixés déjà, trop spéciaux, pour donner l'ébauche molle d'une nature si

has not yet conquered and exploited. Melville, however, is for the world's oceans what Homer is for the eastern Mediterranean. Melville wrote the story of the great whale, Moby Dick, and of his hunter, of Captain Ahab, in a powerful tale *Moby Dick* (1851)[37] and with it composed the greatest epic of the ocean as an element.[38]

When I here occasionally say whale-fish instead of whale and occasionally say whale-fish hunter instead of whale hunter, I indeed know well that this will be seen as a mode of expression, which is that of a lay person and imprecise. One will instruct me concerning the zoological nature of the whale, which is, as every schoolchild knows, a mammal and not a fish. One could already read in print in old Linnaeus's "System of Nature"[39] from 1776 that the whale-fish has warm blood,

---

différente. Ils avaient poussé loin, presque épuisé, la fécondité de leurs genres. Dans ce cas, les aînés périssent; et c'est très-bas, chez les cadets obscurs de quelque classe parente, que surgit la série nouvelle qui montera plus haut. (V. nos notes.) L'homme leur fit, non un fils, mais un frère,—un frère cruellement ennemi. Le voilà arrivé, le fort des forts, l'ingénieux, l'actif, *le cruel roi du monde*. Mon livre s'illumine. Mais aussi que va-t-il montrer? Et que de choses tristes il me faut maintenant amener dans cette lumière ! Ce créateur, ce Dieu tyran, il a su faire une seconde nature dans la nature" (emphasis added on the words that Schmitt appears to quote in the passage above). Jules Michelet, *La mer*, 2nd ed. (Paris: Librairie de L. Hachette, 1861), bk. 2, ch. 13, p. 258.

37. In the 1942, 1954, and 1981 editions of *Land und Meer*, Schmitt places "Moby Dick" in quotation marks rather than italics, but the title of the work is placed in italics above to conform with English convention. Cf. Schmitt (1942), p. 19; Schmitt (1954), p. 16; Schmitt (1981), p. 30. In Fernandez-Quintanilla's 1952 Spanish translation, *Tierra y Mar*, the title *Moby Dick* is placed in italics, as it is in Giovanni Gurisatti's 2002 Italian translation, *Terra e Mare* (Milan: Adelphi Edizioni, 2002). Cf. Schmitt, *Tierra y Mar* (1952), p. 30; Schmitt, *Terra e Mare* (2002), p. 32.

38. In a letter to Ernst Jünger dated July 4, 1941, Schmitt writes: "*Moby Dick* is, as *epos* of the sea, only to be compared with the *Odyssey*. The sea as an element can only be grasped via Melville." Jünger–Schmitt, *Briefe 1930–1983*, p. 121.

39. Schmitt here refers to the 1776 supplement to Carl Linnaeus's (1707–1778) work *Systema naturae*, the first edition of which was published in 1735. Schmitt gives the title of the work in German (rather than Latin) in quotation

breathes through lungs and not, like a fish, through gills, that the female whale-fish brings live offspring in a highly developed state into the world, and that it lovingly nurses and cares for its offspring for almost a year. In no way do I desire to quarrel with the scholars of the profound science of the whale, the cetologists, but only, without any self-righteousness, briefly explain why I do not wholly shy away from the old name, whale-fish. The whale is self-evidently not a fish like a herring or a pike. But in nonetheless calling this curious monster a fish, I express the astonishment that resides in the fact that such a warm-blooded giant is handed over to the element of the sea without its physical endowment fitting it for the sea. Picture for yourself just once the inverse case, that a gigantic life form breathing through its gills were to saunter about upon firm land! The largest, strongest, most powerful sea animal, which swims through the world's seas from the North Pole to the South Pole, breathes through lungs, and, as a mammal, puts living offspring into this sea world! Nor is it an amphibian, but rather an authentic mammal and yet simultaneously, according to the element in which it lives, a fish. And the hunters of this gigantic fish were in the period with which we are here concerned, namely, from the sixteenth to the nineteenth centuries, really hunters in the grand style, not mere "catchers." This is not without significance for our theme.

Michelet, the French encomiast of the whale, describes in his book on the sea the love and the family life of whale-fish with particular tenderness. The male whale-fish is the most knightly lover of the female whale, the most tender mate, the most caring father. He is the most humane of all life-forms, more humane than the human, who drives him to extinction with barbaric cruelty. But how harmless were the methods of whale

---

marks. On Linnaeus, see Ernst Jünger's letter to Schmitt dated March 3, 1941, in Jünger–Schmitt, *Briefe 1930–1983*, p. 116.

catching at the time when Michelet wrote this, although even then steamships and cannons made the weaponry unequal and degraded the poor whale into an object of easy target practice. What would Michelet, amicable toward animals and humans, say now if he were to see the contemporary state of industrialized extraction of whale oil and the industrialized liquidation of whale corpses! Indeed, one can no longer designate as hunting, and hardly even as catching, that which today, after the World War of 1914–1918, has developed under the name of "pelagic" whaling. Today there sail grand ships, weighing up to 30,000 tons, equipped with electrical machines, cannons, grenades, airplanes, and radios, like swimming factories in the Ice Sea at the South Pole. There the whale had fled, and there the dead animal is industrially processed promptly aboard ship. Thus, the poor Leviathan has almost disappeared from our planet. In the years 1937 and 1938, an international convention was finally reached that sets certain regulations for whale killing, divides the fields of capture, and offers similar precautions, so that at least the still living remnant can be protected from further unplanned extinction.[40]

By contrast, the whale hunters, who are here under discussion, were real hunters, not mere catchers, and, certainly, not mechanized whale slaughterers. From the North Sea or from the coast of the Atlantic, they followed their game through the vast spaces of the world's seas with sailing vessels or oar-drawn boats, and the weapon with which they took up this battle against the powerful and clever sea giant was a harpoon flung from the human arm. This was a life-endangering battle

40. Schmitt here apparently makes reference to the *International Agreement for the Regulation of Whaling*, signed in London in June 1937, and its successor convention, *The Protocol Extending the International Agreement for the Regulation of Whaling of 8 June 1937 to after 30 June 1938*, signed in London in June 1938, to which the governments of the United States of America, Canada, Germany, the United Kingdom of Great Britain and Northern Ireland, Ireland, the United States of Mexico, New Zealand, and Norway were parties.

between two life-forms, both of which, without being fish in the zoological sense of the word, moved in the element of the sea. All the aids that the human deployed in this battle were serviced by human muscle power: sail, oar, and the deadly projectile, the harpoon. The whale was strong enough to smash boat and ship with a single smack of its tail. The whale knew how to oppose human trickery with a thousand tricks of its own. Herman Melville, who himself spent multiple years as a sailor aboard a whale-fish hunting ship, sketches in his *Moby Dick*[41] how here there enters what one could call a personal relationship and an inner, enemy–friend bond between the hunter and his game. Here, the human is driven ever further into the elementary depths of maritime existence, through its battle with the other life-form of the sea.

These whale-fish hunters sailed from the north to the south of the terrestrial orb and from the Atlantic to the Pacific Ocean. Always following the secretive trails of the whales, they discovered islands and continents, without making much ado about it. In Melville, when one of these seafarers becomes acquainted with the book of Captain Cook, the discoverer of Australia, the seafarer says: This Cook writes books about things that a whale hunter would never write in his log book.[42] Who, Michelet asks,

---

41. In the 1942, 1954, and 1981 editions of *Land und Meer*, Schmitt places "Moby Dick" in quotation marks rather than italics, but the title of the work is placed in italics above to conform with English convention. Cf. Schmitt (1942), p. 22; Schmitt (1954), p. 18; Schmitt (1981), p. 33. In Fernandez-Quintanilla's 1952 Spanish translation, *Tierra y Mar*, the title *Moby Dick* is placed in italics, as it is in Gurisatti's 2002 Italian translation, *Terra e Mare*. Cf. Schmitt, *Tierra y Mar* (1952), p. 34; Schmitt, *Terra e Mare* (2002), p. 35.

42. Schmitt here appears to refer to (or, rather, to quote freely from) part of Ishmael's narration in ch. 24 ("The Advocate") of Herman Melville's *Moby Dick*: "I freely assert, that the cosmopolite philosopher cannot, for his life, point out one single peaceful influence, which within the last sixty years has operated more potentially upon the whole broad world, taken in one aggregate, than the high and mighty business of whaling. One way and another, it has begotten events so remarkable in themselves, and so continuously

revealed the ocean to humans? Who discovered the zones and lanes of the ocean? In a word: who discovered the globe? The whale and the whale-fish hunter! And all of this independent of Columbus and the famed seekers of gold, who only discovered, with great noise, what the fishing races from the North, from Bretagne and from the Basque country, had already discovered. Michelet says all this and proceeds to say: These whale-fish hunters are the most sublime expression of human courage. Without the whale-fish, the fishers would always have only kept to the coasts. The whale lured them onto the oceans and emancipated them from the coasts. Through the whale one discovered the sea currents and found the Northwest Passage. The whale-fish led us.

At that time, in the sixteenth century, there stood upon our planet simultaneously two different kinds of hunters in an

---

momentous in their sequential issues, that whaling may well be regarded as that Egyptian mother, who bore offspring themselves pregnant from her womb. It would be a hopeless, endless task to catalogue all these things. Let a handful suffice. For many years past the whale-ship has been the pioneer in ferreting out the remotest and least known parts of the earth. She had explored seas and archipelagos which had no chart, where no Cook or Vancouver had ever sailed. If American and European men-of-war now peacefully ride in once savage harbors, let them fire salutes to the honor and the glory of the whale-ship, which originally showed them the way, and first interpreted between them and the savages. They may celebrate as they will the heroes of Exploring Expeditions, your Cooks, your Krusensterns; but I say that scores of anonymous Captains have sailed out of Nantucket, that were as great, and greater than your Cook and your Krusenstern. For in their succorless empty-handedness, they, in the heathenish sharked waters, and by the beaches of unrecorded javelin islands, battled with virgin wonders and terrors that Cook with all his marines and muskets would not willingly have dared. All that is made such a flourish of in the old South Sea Voyages, those things were but the life-time commonplaces of our heroic Nantucketers. Often, adventures which Vancouver dedicates three chapters to, these men accounted unworthy of being set down in the ship's common log. Ah, the world! Oh, the world!" Herman Melville, *Moby Dick, or The Whale* (New York: Penguin Books, 2001 [1851]), ch. 24, pp. 119–20.

elementary rupture. Both opened new, infinite spaces, out of which great empires emerged. By land the Russian pelt hunters, who, following furred animals, conquered Siberia by land paths and reached the eastern coast of Asia; by sea these northern and western European whale hunters, who hunted through all the world's seas and, as Michelet rightly says, made the globe visible. They are the first-born of a new elementary existence, the first new, real "children of the sea."[43]

6

In this pivotal period, an important technological event occurs. Here, too, the Dutch are on top. Around 1600, they were the uncontested masters of shipbuilding. They invented the new sail technology and the new types of sailing ship, which surpassed the oar and made possible a new mode of sea travel and navigation corresponding to the size of the newly discovered world oceans.

Departing from the West Frisian city of Hoorn in Northern Holland in 1595, a new type of ship emerged, a boat with yard sails, which did not sail like the old sails simply with tailwinds, but rather sailed sideward into the winds and which could utilize the wind in a manner wholly different from that of the traditional sail. The rigging and the art of sailing were now perfected in an unforeseen way. "In a catastrophic manner medieval seafaring collapses," Bernhard Hagedorn, the historiographer of the development of types of ship, says of this event.[44] Here lies the actual turning point in the history of the relation between land and sea. Whatever was possible to create with the material, out of which at that time ship and rigging

43. Cf. Hosea 11:10 in the Latin Vulgate.
44. A reference to Bernhard Hagedorn (1882–1914) and his 1914 work *Die Entwicklung der wichtigsten Schiffstypen bis ins 19. Jh.* (*The Development of the Most Important Types of Ship up into the Nineteenth Century*) (Berlin: Curtius, 1914).

were composed, was achieved. Only in the nineteenth century did another revolution in the domain of shipbuilding technology take place. "It must have been like a revelation," Hagedorn claims, "for the skippers, when they gave up on the large sail and saw how much they could accomplish with the small one." Through this technological achievement, the Dutch became the "cart people" of all European lands. They also became the heirs to the trade of the German Hanseatic League. Even the world power of Spain had to rent Dutch ships to be able to maintain its overseas traffic.

In the sixteenth century the new warship also emerged, and with it there begins a new epoch of waging naval warfare. A gun-laden sailing ship would be equipped with cannons on its broadside and would fire salvos from its broadside at the opponent. Sea battle thereby became an artillery battle from afar conducted with the highest art of sailing. Only now can one really speak of a sea battle, while, as we saw, the battle for the occupation of oared galleys is only a land battle aboard ship. A wholly new tactics for sea battle and for conducting sea war is bound up with this, a new, high art of the "evolutions," which before, during, and after the sea battle are necessary. The first scientific book, in the modern sense, about this new art stems from a Frenchman, the Jesuit father Paul Hoste, and appeared in Lyon in 1697 under the title *L'art des armées navales ou traité des évolutions navales*.[45] In a critical manner, it treats sea

---

45. Schmitt here appears to refer to Paul Hoste's (1652–1700) text *L'art des armées navales, ou traité des évolutions navales, qui contient des règles utiles aux officiers généraux, & particuliers d'une armée navale; avec des exemples tirez de ce qui s'est passé de plus considérable sur la mer depuis cinquante ans* (*The Art of Naval Armies, or [a] treatise on naval evolutions, which contains useful rules for officers generally, and particularly for officers of a naval army; with examples drawn from the most considerable things which have happened at sea during the past fifty years*) (Lyon: Anisson & Posuel, 1697). The title page of the 1697 edition of Hoste's treatise claims that the work was published with royal privilege.

battles and sea maneuvers of the Dutch, the English, and the French during the wars of Louis XIV against the Dutch. Other French works followed. Only in the eighteenth century, in 1782, with Clerk d'Eldin,[46] does an Englishman enter the ranks of renowned theoreticians of sea tactics.

All western and middle European peoples had their part in the collective achievement, which lay in the discovery of a new earth and which led to European rule over the world. Italians perfected the compass and drew maps of the seas; the discovery of America is owed, above all, to the thinking and to the force of the knowledge of Toscanelli and Columbus. The Portuguese and Spanish undertook the first great voyages of discovery and circumnavigated the earth. Great German astronomers and exceptional geographers contributed to the new view of the world; a German cosmographer, Waltzemüller, invented the name "America" (1507),[47] and the Welser enterprise in Venezuela was a great colonial project, which, admittedly, could not overcome the Spanish resistance.[48] The Dutch were leaders in

46. Schmitt here appears to refer to John Clerk of Eldin (1728–1812), whose work *An Inquiry into Naval Tactics* was privately published in Edinburgh in 1782, according to the catalogues of the Bodleian Library. According to the *Oxford Dictionary of National Biography*, Eldin was born in Edinburgh. Schmitt appears to have rendered John Clerk of Eldin in French form as "Clerk d'Eldin," as if this author were French.

47. Martin Waltzemüller (ca. 1470–75 to ca. 1520–21) (alt: Martin Waldseemüller; Martin Waldenseemüller; Martinus Ilacomilus) was a German cartographer. Waltzemüller's 1507 map *Universalis Cosmographia Secundum Ptholomaei Traditionem et Americi Vespucii Alioru[m]que Lustrationes*, to which Schmitt appears to refer in the passage above, is credited with coining the term "America" by assigning the term on his map to the Trans-Atlantic lands encountered by Europeans in the late fifteenth and early sixteenth centuries. A copy of Waltzemüller's *Universalis Cosmographia* is held in the collections of the Library of Congress.

48. Partially through forgiveness of debts, the Augsburg-based Welser banking family purchased claims of colonization and exploration in Venezuela from the Holy Roman Emperor Charles V (King Charles I of Spain), formalized in contracts of February and March 1528. Through a mixture of

whaling and in the technology of shipbuilding. France had particularly great potential, both due to its geographic position on three coasts—on the Mediterranean, on the Atlantic Ocean, and on the Channel—through its economic riches and through the seafarer spirit of the population on its Atlantic coast. A French Viking, Jean Fleury, led the first great attack against the Spanish world power in 1522 and took away two ships laden with treasures, which Cortez had sent from America to Spain; a French discoverer, Jean Cartier, already in 1540 found Canada, the "new France," and seized it as a possession for his king. Huguenot corsairs, who swarmed out of La Rochelle, represented a particularly important contingent in the eruption of maritime energies of this time. Under the ingenious naval secretary Colbert, France still outstripped the English in the construction of warships for many decades in the seventeenth century.

The seafaring achievements of the English are, as is self-evident, in any case significant. But only after 1570 do English seafarers first sail south across the equator. Only in the final third of the sixteenth century does the great breach of the English corsairs on oceanic and American voyages begin.

7

Sea dogs of all kinds, pirates, corsairs, sea-trade-practicing adventurers, compose, alongside the whale hunters and the sailors, the advance column of the elementary turn to the sea, which takes place in the sixteenth and seventeenth centuries. Here we have a further, daring kind of "children of the

slave labor, imperial misadventure, and colonial monopoly, the Welser family exploited its claim to the land and resources of Venezuela from the 1520s to the 1550s. On these exploits see Konrad Haebler, *Die überseeischen Unternehmungen der Welser und ihrer Gesellschafter* (Leipzig: Verlag von C. L. Hirschfeld, 1903); Götz Freiherr von Pölnitz, "Der Kaiser und seine Augsburger Bankiers," in Hubert Freiherr von Welser, Götz Freiherr von Pölnitz, and Peter Strieder, *Bartholomäus Welser und seine Zeit* (Augsburg: Augsburger Druck- und Verlagshaus, 1962), pp. 29–58.

sea."[49] Among them there are famous names, heroes of sea stories and stories of thieves, like Francis Drake, Hawkins, Sir Walter Raleigh, or Sir Henry Morgan, who are exalted in many books, and the life of each of them was, in fact, adventurous enough. They preyed upon Spanish fleets carrying silver, and that in itself is indeed a rousing theme. There is a voluminous literature about pirates in general and many individual great names in particular, and in English one has even put together a lexicon of them under the humorous title "The Pirate's Who's Who,"[50] the pirate's address book.[51]

Whole categories of these daring sea robbers have, however, also achieved real historical fame, because they struck the first blows toward dislodging the Spanish world power and the Spanish monopoly on trade. Thus, the Huguenot pirates in the French sea fort La Rochelle, together with the Dutch "Sea Beggars" fought against Spain in the time of Queen Elizabeth. Then came the so-called Elizabethan corsairs, who made an essential contribution to the annihilation of the Spanish Armada (1588). The corsairs of Queen Elizabeth were followed by those of King James I, among them Sir Henry Mainwaring, at first one of the worst pirates, then pardoned by the King in 1616, and finally a pirate-fighter distinguished with offices and honors. Then there come *Flibustiers* and the wild Buccaneers,[52] who from Jamaica and the Caribbean Sea undertook their great maneuvers, French, Dutch, and English, among them Sir Henry Morgan, who plundered Panama in 1671, was

49. Cf. Hosea 11:10 in the Latin Vulgate.
50. "The Pirate's Who's Who" is English in Schmitt's German original, with partial German orthography (no apostrophe after the "o" in "Who's"—rendered as "Whos Who"), which is modified in the translation above.
51. Schmitt here appears to refer to Philip Gosse's (1879–1959) work of 1924, *The Pirates' Who's Who, Giving the Particulars of the Lives and Deaths of Pirates and Buccaneers* (Boston: Lauriat, 1924).
52. "Flibustiers" and "Buccaneers" are, respectively, French and English in Schmitt's German original.

knighted by King Charles II and became Royal Governor of Jamaica. Their last heroic act was the conquest of the Spanish sea fort Cartagena in Columbia, which they seized together with the French Royal Fleet in 1697 and which, after the French withdrew, they plundered in the most terrible way.

The element of the sea breaks through in these sea dogs. Their heroic period lasted around 150 years, roughly from 1550 until 1713, i.e., from the beginning of the battle of the Protestant powers against the Catholic world power of Spain up until the Peace of Utrecht. At all times and in all seas there have been sea robbers, beginning with the pirates, already mentioned,[53] who were expelled from the eastern Mediterranean several millennia ago by the Cretan Empire, up to the Chinese junks, which still hijacked and plundered trading ships in east Asian waters around 1920 and 1930. But the corsairs of the sixteenth and seventeenth centuries signify a particular phase in the history of piracy. Their time first ends with the Peace of Utrecht (1713), when the European state system consolidated. The war fleets of the sea powers could now exert real control, and England's new world dominion erected upon the seas became visible for the first time. Into the nineteenth century, there were indeed still private corsairs conducting war with the permission of their governments. But the organization of the world progressed, the technologies of shipbuilding and navigation were perfected and became ever more scientific, and piracy is now, as an English marine specialist has said, a "pre-scientific stage of conducting war at sea."[54] The pirate swarming out of his own accord and

53. In section 3 of *Land and Sea*, p. 16, above.
54. Here, Schmitt may be referring to a quote that he elsewhere attributes to the British naval historian and geostrategist Sir Julian Corbett (1854–1922), "the author of *Some principles of maritime strategy*." Cf. Carl Schmitt, *Das internationalrechtliche Verbrechen des Angriffskrieges und der Grundsatz "Nullum crimen, nulla poena sine lege"*, ed. Helmut Quaritsch (Berlin: Duncker & Humblot, 1994), p. 54; Carl Schmitt, "The International Crime of the War of

on his own account has now become a sad criminal. Admittedly, there were always a few exceptions. Among them belongs the French Captain Misson, who, around 1720 in Madagascar, attempted to construct a curious Empire of Humanity. On the whole, however, since the Peace of Utrecht, the pirate has been hurled to the outermost shore of world history. In the eighteenth century, the pirate is now only a dissolute subject, a criminal type of the rawest kind, who can indeed be a figure of thrilling stories like Stevenson's *Treasure Island*, but no longer plays any historical role.

By contrast, the corsairs of the sixteenth and seventeenth centuries play a great historical role. They stand as active fighters in the grand world-historical confrontation between England and Spain. When they were caught, they were marked and hung as common criminals and thieving murderers by their enemies, the Spanish. Even their own government let them fall in cold blood when they became incommodious or when the cautions of external politics demanded it. Often, it was really an accident whether such a corsair ended as a bearer

---

Aggression and the Principle '*Nullum crimen, nulla poena sine lege*' (1945)," in *Writings on War*, ed. Timothy Nunan (Cambridge: Polity Press, 2011), p. 168: "A sentence from the author of 'principles of maritime strategy,' Sir Julian Corbett, clarifies this important parallel better than any juridical discussion: 'piracy is the pre-scientific stage of the conducting of naval war.' Through this statement it becomes clear what the parallel of war and piracy really means." Schmitt's source for this quotation may be Julian Corbett's 1911 treatise (reissued in a new edition in 1918) *Some Principles of Maritime Strategy*, in which Corbett writes: "The idea of privateering was a survival of a primitive and unscientific conception of war, which was governed mainly by a general notion of doing your enemy as much damage as possible and making reprisal for wrongs he had done you. To the same class of ideas belonged the practice of plunder and ravaging ashore. But neither of these methods of war was abolished for humanitarian reasons. They disappeared indeed as a general practice before the world had begun to talk of humanity. They were abolished because war became more scientific." Julian S. Corbett, *Some Principles of Maritime Strategy*, new ed. (London: Longmans, Green, and Co., 1918), pp. 81–82.

of regal honors or ended on the gallows as a pirate condemned to death. In addition, the different labels, like pirate, corsair, privateers, merchant-adventurer,[55] were, in practice, unclearly and interchangeably deployed. Seen juristically, in itself, there is a great distinction between pirates and corsairs. The corsair has, in contrast with the pirate, a legal title, an empowerment from his government, a formal letter of marque and reprisal from his king. He may fly the flag of his country. By contrast, the pirate sails without legal mandate. For him, only the black pirate flag is appropriate. But as fine and clear as this distinction may be in theory, it dissolves in practice. The corsairs often overstepped the bounds of their mandates and sailed with false letters of marque and reprisal, sometimes also with forged letters of empowerment from non-existing governments.[56]

There is something more essential than such juristic questions. All these Rochellois, Sea Beggars, and Buccaneers[57] had a political enemy, namely, the Catholic world power of Spain. As long as they held something of themselves, they fundamentally only captured Catholic ships, and saw this in good conscience as work pleasing to God, as work blessed by God. They thus stood in a great world-historical front of what was then World Protestantism against what was then World Catholicism. On this account, one need not beautify the fact that they murdered, scorched, and plundered. In the complete situation of this pivotal time, in any case, they have their position and, with it, their historical significance and their historical rank.

---

55. In Schmitt's text "privateers" and "merchant-adventurer" are in English in the German original.

56. In the first two editions of *Land and Sea*, this clause began "sometimes also with finely forged [*schön verbrieften*] letters of empowerment from non-existing governments." In the 1981 edition, the "finely" (*schön*) was omitted. Schmitt (1942), p. 30; Schmitt (1954), p. 25; Schmitt (1981), p. 44.

57. "Rochellois" (i.e., persons from La Rochelle) and "Buccaneers" are, respectively, in French and English in Schmitt's German original.

## 8

The world-historical consciousness of the English monarchs—whether Queen Elizabeth or the Stuarts James and Charles—and the English statesmen of this period was not different from that of most of their contemporaries. They made their policies, took those advantages that presented themselves, pocketed the profits, and sought to hold every position. They applied the law, when they had it on their side, and protested indignantly against injustice, when this was on the side of their opponents. This is all wholly natural. Their notions of God and world and law and their consciousness of the world-historical developments that were being set in motion were—aside from ingenious exceptions like Thomas More[58] or Cardinal Wolsey or Francis Bacon—in no way more modern than the notions of most statesmen and diplomats of any other European country that was involved in high politics.

Queen Elizabeth is freely held as the great founder of English rule of the seas, and this fame is also well-deserved. She began the battle with the Catholic world power of Spain. Under her government, the Spanish Armada was vanquished in the channel (1588); she honored and encouraged sea heroes like Francis Drake and Walter Raleigh; from her hand the English East India Company, which later conquered all of India for England, received its trading privilege in the year 1600. In the forty-five years of her government (1558 to 1603), England became a rich country, which it had not been previously. Previously, the English had herded sheep and sold the wool to Flanders; now, however, the fabled loot of English corsairs and pirates flowed from all seas to the English island. The Queen

---

58. Schmitt preserves the Latinized version of More's name, as "Thomas Morus," as this is the standard spelling of More's name in German texts (and the spelling of More's name in works that More himself published in his lifetime). The standard English spelling has been given in the translation above.

rejoiced in these treasures and enriched herself with them. In this respect, in all her virginal innocence, she did nothing other than what numerous noble and bourgeois Englishmen and Englishwomen of her time did. They all took part in the great business of loot. Hundreds and thousands of Englishmen and Englishwomen at that time became "corsair capitalists."[59] This, too, belongs to the elementary turn from the land to the sea, of which we are here speaking.

A fine example of this flowering period of early predatory capitalism is offered to us by the Killigrew family of Cornwall. From their way of life and their world image we receive a more lively and more correct picture of the then leading classes and the true "elite," than from official reports and from many time-bound written works, formulated in the official style. These Killigrews are typical of their time in a manner wholly different from that of most diplomats, jurists, and laurel-crowned poets, although it is in any case worth noting that among them named intellectuals are to be found and today the name Killigrew is still represented more than ten times in England's *Dictionary of National Biography*.[60] Let us thus linger a moment with this highly interesting elite.[61]

---

59. "Corsair capitalists" is in English in Schmitt's German original with partial German orthography, and is preceded by a German translation of the term in quotation marks ("zu 'Korsaren-Kapitalisten,' zu corsairs capitalists"). Schmitt (1981), p. 46. The repetition has been removed and the German orthography modified in the English translation above ("corsair capitalists" in place of "corsairs capitalists").

60. Schmitt here appears to refer to the first edition of the *Dictionary of National Biography*, published in sixty-three volumes from 1885–1900, under the editorships of Leslie Stephen (1885–91) and Sidney Lee (1891–1900), reissued with many supplements throughout the twentieth century.

61. The last sentence of this paragraph in the German original ("Verweilen wir also einen Augenblick...") seems to contain a reference to a famous passage in Goethe's *Faust I*, where Faust wishes for a beautiful moment to linger ("Werd' ich zum Augenblick sagen / Verweile doch! Du bist so schön"),

The Killigrew family sat in Arwenack in Cornwall (southwestern England). The head of the family in the time of Queen Elizabeth was Sir John Killigrew, vice-admiral of Cornwall and hereditary royal governor of Pendennis Castle. He worked in the closest association with William Cecil, Lord Burleigh, the first minister of the Queen.[62] The father and uncle of the vice-admiral had already been pirates, and even against his mother there was, as writers of English history credibly inform us, a legal case concerning piracy introduced in court. One part of the family worked on the English coast, another part in Ireland, numerous cousins and further clan members on the coasts of Devon and Dorset.[63] In addition, they had friends and cronies of all kinds. They organized the hijackings and raids, ambushed the ships that approached their coasts, oversaw the division of

---

thus sealing his pact with Mephistopheles (Goethe, *Faust I*, ll. 1699–1700ff.). Schmitt (1981), p. 47.

62. One potential source for Schmitt's writing on the Killigrew family in this passage is Philip Gosse's *The History of Piracy* (London: Longmans, Green and Co., 1932), pp. 107–8: "By far the greatest of these magnates of piracy were the Killigrews of Cornwall. From this ancient family, which provided many a distinguished minister, diplomat and soldier to the nation, arose a veritable oligarchy of corsair capitalists. The seat of the family was Arwenack in Cornwall and its head in Elizabeth's time was Sir John Killigrew, Vice-Admiral of Cornwall and hereditary Royal Governor of Pendennis Castle, who acted as a sort of managing director of the family business. He was closely connected by blood with William Cecil, Lord Burleigh, the Queen's principal minister." Schmitt had referred to Gosse's 1924 work *The Pirates' Who's Who* in section 7 of *Land and Sea*, above.

63. One potential source for this passage is Gosse's *The History of Piracy*, p. 108: "Sir John's father had been a pirate and his uncle Peter had sailed the Irish Sea as a rover in his younger days. Even his mother, as will appear presently, was to be tried in a court of law for piracy. One of his relatives, Sir John Wogan, Vice-Admiral of South Wales, looked after the family interests on that coast; he too once stood trial for piracy. Another relative, John Godolphin, acted as agent in his own district of Cornwall, while the important base at Tralee in Ireland was in charge of a neighbour of Sir John's, the Vice-President of Munster and member of parliament for Liskard. Various other cousins looked after the branches along the Devon and Dorset coasts."

the loot, and sold shares, posts, and offices. The great house in which the Killigrew family resided in Arwenack stood immediately on the sea in a closed-off part of Falmouth Harbor and had a secret path to the sea. The only building that lay nearby was Pendennis Castle, mentioned above, the seat of the royal governor. It was equipped with 100 cannons and served the pirates in an emergency as a hideout. The noble Lady Killigrew had previously assisted her father, a distinguished "gentleman pirate,"[64] when she became her spouse's able and successful collaborator. She provided for the accommodation of the pirates in their house and was a hospitable housemistress. There were hostels and hideouts set up in all the harbors in the area.[65]

Seldom was the work of the Killigrew family disturbed or even hindered by regal impediments.[66] Only once, in the year 1582, did it come to such a disturbance, which I would

---

64. The phrase "gentleman pirate" is quoted in English in the German original. Cf. Schmitt (1981), p. 48. One potential source for this quotation is Gosse's *The History of Piracy*, p. 110: "It was a mistake in the selection of her victim that finally brought old Lady Killigrew to justice. This extraordinary woman had been assistant to her father, Philip Wolverston, a distinguished gentleman pirate of Suffolk, before becoming a valuable helpmate to her husband."

65. One potential source for this passage is Gosse's *The History of Piracy*, p. 109: "Falmouth was probably as important as any English port for the trading of pirate plunder, for it was the home of the Killigrews. Their great house of Arwenack stood close to the sea in a secluded part of Falmouth Harbour, and had a private and secret way down to the water. Pendennis Castle was the only other building near and although armed with over a hundred cannon it was more a refuge than a menace to visiting pirate ships. At Arwenack Lady Killigrew dispensed hospitality to the more respectable pirates, and the Killigrews' connections did the same at their houses. One notorious pirate chief who worked the Bristol Channel and South Wales made his residence when on shore with the Sergeant of the Admiralty. The syndicate provided rest and comfort for the crews in recognised lodging houses for pirates in the receiving ports."

66. One potential source for this passage is Gosse's *The History of Piracy*, p. 110: "It was very rarely indeed that one of Killigrews' employees was ever seriously interfered with."

like to narrate briefly. A ship of the Hanseatic League weighing 144 tons, which belonged to two Spaniards, was driven into Falmouth Harbor by a storm. As England at that time had peace with Spain, the two Spaniards thoughtlessly dropped anchor, and did so immediately facing the house at Arwenack. Lady Killigrew spotted the ship from her window and with her schooled eye saw immediately that the cargo was composed of valuable Dutch cloth.[67] On the night of January 7, 1582, the armed people of the Killigrews—with the Lady personally in command—hijacked the poor ship, slaughtered the crew, threw the corpses into the sea, and returned to Arwenack with the valuable Dutch cloth and other loot. In an inexplicable manner, the ship itself disappeared to Ireland.[68] With luck, the two owners of the ship, both Spaniards, were not on board, because

---

67. Cf. Gosse, *The History of Piracy*, pp. 110-11: "It was a mistake in the selection of her victim that finally brought old Lady Killigrew to justice. This extraordinary woman had been assistant to her father, Philip Wolverston, a distinguished gentleman pirate of Suffolk, before becoming a valuable helpmate to her husband. But in 1582 she overreached herself. On New Year's Day a Hansa ship of a hundred and forty-four tons burden was driven into Falmouth harbour by a storm. She dropped anchor directly opposite Arwenack—since the house was the residence of the Commissioner of Piracy for Cornwall and since England was at peace with the world, the master might reasonably think that he had nothing to fear. But from her drawing-room window her ladyship noticed the foreign vessel, made enquiries and learnt that there was valuable merchandise on board. In the meantime the owners of the vessel, two Spanish gentlemen, Philip de Orozo and Juan de Charis, had gone to Penryn to stop at the inn until the weather turned favourable."

68. Cf. Gosse, *The History of Piracy*, p. 111: "On the night of January 7th a boat put off from shore filled with armed retainers of Sir John Killigrew and steered by Lady Killigrew herself. On coming alongside, the Cornishmen, headed by her ladyship, scrambled on deck, slaughtered the unsuspecting crew and threw their bodies over the side. Lady Killigrew and two of her servants, Kendal and Hawkins, returned to Arwenack with several bolts of holland cloth and two barrels of pieces of eight, while the Cornish sailors took the captured ship to Ireland where the rest of the plunder was disposed of."

they had spent the night in a small hotel on land. They brought a case before the English court with jurisdiction in Cornwall. After several investigations, the court came to the finding that the ship was probably stolen by persons unknown and, incidentally, the circumstances of the case could no longer be ascertained.[69] However, as both Spaniards chanced to have political connections, they managed to have their suits brought to the highest court in London, so that a new investigation was ordered. Lady Killigrew was brought to court together with her collaborators in another locality. She was found guilty and condemned to death. Two of her assistants were executed, the Lady herself pardoned at the last minute.[70]

So much for the true history of Lady Killigrew. Even in the fourteenth year of the reign of Queen Elizabeth, the greater part of English tonnage was in transit on voyages of plunder or in illegal business activities, and hardly more than 50,000 tons sailed conducting legal trade. The Killigrews are a fine example for the home front of the great Age of Sea Robbers, in which an old English prophecy from the thirteenth century was fulfilled: "The children of the lion shall be transformed into fish of the sea."[71] Now, at the end of the Middle Ages, the children of the

69. Cf. Gosse, *The History of Piracy*, p. 111: "The owners at once laid formal complaint before the Commissioners of Piracy in Cornwall, of which the offender's son was president. After enquiry it was found that there was no evidence to implicate any known persons. The jury returned an open verdict: the ship had certainly been stolen, but by whom they found it impossible to say."

70. Cf. Gosse, *The History of Piracy*, p. 111: "Charis and Arozo were persistent, however. They went up to London and laid their complaint before the highest authorities, with the result that the Earl of Bedford, a member of the Privy Council, instructed Sir Richard Grenville and Mr. Edmund Tremayne to conduct a searching investigation into the affair. At the conclusion of their enquiry Lady Killigrew, Hawkins and Kendal were duly found guilty and condemned to death. The two men were executed but Lady Killigrew received a reprieve at the last moment."

71. Schmitt seems here to quote from Percy Ernst Schramm's 1937 history of English coronation rites, *Geschichte des englischen Königtums im*

lion mainly herded sheep, whose wool was turned into cloth in Flanders. Only in the sixteenth and seventeenth centuries was this people of shepherds first really transformed into a people of sea dogs and corsairs, into "children of the sea."[72]

9

The oceanic seafaring achievements of the English set in relatively late and slowly. The Portuguese had traveled the world for more than one hundred years, although, admittedly, mostly only along the coasts. From 1492, the Spanish followed with the great Conquista, the conquest of America. French seafarers, the Huguenots, and the English followed close behind. But only in 1553, with the founding of the Muscovy Company,[73] does England first begin an overseas policy that to a certain extent brings it on par with the other colonial world powers. As was already mentioned,[74] only after 1570 do the English sail south

---

*Lichte der Krönung* (Weimar: Hermann Böhlaus, 1937), p. 124. Schmitt had deployed this quotation in two articles from 1941 that sketch earlier versions of the argument of *Land and Sea*, "Das Meer gegen das Land" ("The Sea against the Land"), published in the journal *Das Reich*, on March 9, 1941, and in the longer lecture and article "Staatliche Souveränität und freies Meer: Über den Gegensatz von Land und See im Völkerrecht der Neuzeit" ("State Sovereignty and Free Sea: On the Opposition between Land and Sea in the Law of Peoples of the Early Modern Period"), delivered as a lecture at a history conference in Nuremberg held on February 7–8, 1941, and printed in the collection *Das Reich und Europa* (*The Reich and Europe*) (Leipzig: 1941), the latter of which cites Schramm's text with bibliographic information. Both articles are reprinted in Schmitt, *Staat, Großraum, Nomos*, pp. 395–400, 397, 401–30, 409n7.

72. Cf. Hosea 11:10 in the Latin Vulgate: "post Dominum ambulabunt quasi leo rugiet quia ipse rugiet et formidabunt filii maris." Hosea 11:10 is rendered in the Douay-Rheims translation as follows: "They shall walk after the Lord, he shall roar as a lion: because he shall roar, and the children of the sea shall fear."

73. "Muscovy Company" is in English in Schmitt's German text.

74. In the last paragraph of section 6 of *Land and Sea*.

of the equator. The first practical document in which England begins to set itself a new English world horizon is the book by Hakluyt, *Principal Navigations*; it appeared in 1589. Even in whaling and shipbuilding, the Dutch were, as they were for other peoples, the teachers of the English.

Nonetheless it was the English who finally overtook everyone, vanquished all rivals, and attained a world domination erected upon the domination of the oceans. England became the heir. It was the heir to the great hunters and sailors, the researchers and discoverers of all other European peoples. What was attained in maritime achievements and bold acts of seafaring by German, Dutch, Norwegian, and Danish seafarers at that time, finally flowed into British maritime domination over the earth. Indeed, great colonial empires of other European peoples continued to stand. Portugal and Spain held gigantic overseas possessions, but they lost dominion over the sea and the lines of transport. When Cromwell occupied and held Jamaica in 1655, England's complete orientation to world-oceanic and political empire and its overseas victory over Spain were decided. Holland, which attained the high point of its maritime activity around 1600, was already a hundred years later, around 1700, sharply confined to land. It had to defend itself on land against Louis XIV and had to erect strong land fortifications; its stadtholder William III of Orange simultaneously became King of England in 1689; he removed himself to the island and made English policy; no longer did he make policy for Holland on its own. France did not persevere in its great attempt for the sea, which was bound up with Huguenot Protestantism. Its spiritual tradition lay ultimately in a Roman line, and when it had decided against the Huguenots and for Catholicism, with the Night of Bartholomew in 1572 and the conversion of Henri IV to Catholicism, it ultimately had decided against the sea and for the land. Admittedly, as we have seen,[75] the maritime forces of France were still very great under Louis XV and could have stood up against England. However, after the French king released his great marine minister and minister of trade, Colbert, the decision for the land was no longer reversible. The long colonial battles of the eighteenth century only confirmed this. Germany's share, however, was lost in the Wars of Religion and in the misery of the Empire of that time.

Thus England became the heir, the universal heir of this great upheaval of the European peoples. How was this possible? It cannot be explained through comparisons with earlier historical examples of maritime dominion, nor through parallels with Athens or Carthage, Rome, Byzantium, or Venice. Here lies a case unique in its essence. Its uniqueness, its incomparability, consists in the fact that England completed an elementary transformation in a wholly other historical moment and in a manner fully different from any other sea power. It really displaced its existence away from the land and into the element of the sea. It thereby won not only sea battles and wars but also something wholly other and infinitely greater, namely, a revolution, and, indeed, a revolution of the greatest kind, a planetary spatial revolution.

## 10

A spatial revolution—what is this?

The human receives a particular historical consciousness from his "space," which is subjected to great historical transformations. The variegated forms of life correspond to equally differentiated spaces. Even within the same time period, the environment of individual humans for the practice of daily life is already defined differently by their different life

---

75. This appears to be a cross-reference to the penultimate and antepenultimate paragraphs of section 6 of *Land and Sea*.

occupations. An urbanite thinks the world otherwise than does a peasant farmer, a whale-fish hunter has another living space [*Lebensraum*][76] than an opera singer, and to a pilot the world and life appear otherwise not only in other lights but also in other quantities, depths, and horizons. The differences between spatial conceptions are still deeper and greater when it is a matter of different peoples and different periods of human history.

The scientific doctrines of space could mean here, in practice, very much and very little. For hundreds of years the few learned people who at that time already regarded the earth as a sphere were held to be vermin and spiritually sick. In modernity, the different sciences also worked out their separate spatial conceptions with increasing specialization. Geometry, physics, psychology, and biology here go their own ways, diverging widely from one another. If you ask the learned, they shall reply to you that mathematic space is something wholly other than the space of an electromagnetic force field and this space again wholly different from space in the psychological and biological senses. There are a half-dozen concepts of space. Here, any unity is lacking, and the danger lurks that the great problem will be defrayed and destroyed by too much talk through the unrelated coexistence of different concepts. Even the philosophy and epistemology of the nineteenth century gave us no comprehensive, simple answer [to the great question of space] and, in practice, left us in the lurch.

76. While Schmitt here deploys the term "Lebensraum" to describe different spatial orientations, he would later claim, in his 1947 interrogations at Nuremberg, that the term "Lebensraum" was inapt to describe his thought in the period 1933–45. Carl Schmitt, *Antworten in Nürnberg*, ed. Helmut Quaritsch (Berlin: Duncker & Humblot, 2000), p. 54: "F. Sie geben aber zu, daß das absolut eine Völkerrechtstheorie des Lebensraumes ist?/A. Ich sage Großraum./F. Hitler war auch für den Großraum./A. Das waren sie wohl alle gewesen, auch Angehörige anderer Staaten." Cf. Carl Schmitt, "Interrogation of Carl Schmitt by Robert Kempner (I)–(III)," trans. Joseph W. Bendersky, *Telos*, no. 72 (Summer 1987), pp. 99–100.

But historical forces and powers do not wait for science, they wait as little as Christopher Columbus waited for Copernicus. Every time when new lands and seas enter the field of vision of human collective consciousness by a new thrust of historical forces, by an unleashing of new energies, the spaces of historical existence also change. Then there emerge new measures and directions of political-historical activity, new sciences, new orders, new life for new or reborn peoples. The expansion can be so deep and so surprising that not only quantities and measurements, not only the outermost human horizon, but even the structure of the concept of space itself is altered. Then one may speak of a spatial revolution. But a transformation of the sense of space is generally a part of each great historical change. That is the authentic core of the encompassing political, economic, and cultural transformation that then transpires.

We can quickly make clear to ourselves this general state of affairs with three historical examples: the consequences of the conquests of Alexander the Great, the Roman Empire in the first century of our era, and the consequences of the Crusades on the development of Europe.

11

In Alexander the Great's maneuvers of conquest, a powerful, new spatial horizon opened to the Greeks. The culture and art of Hellenism is its consequence. Aristotle, the great philosopher,[77] a contemporary of this spatial transformation, already saw that the human-inhabited world drew itself ever

77. In his article on Machiavelli from 1927, Schmitt commented that "the systematic learnedness of the books of Aristotle" ("die systematische Gelehrsamkeit der Bücher des Aristoteles") was one respect in which he regarded the works of Machiavelli as of lesser status than those of Aristotle. Cf. Carl Schmitt, "Macchiavelli, Zum 22. Juni 1927," *Kölnischen Volkszeitung*, June 21, 1927; reprinted in Schmitt, *Staat, Großraum, Nomos*, pp. 102–7.

more together, from the East and from the West. Aristarchus of Samos, who lived slightly later (310–230), already conjectured that the sun is a fixed star, standing in the center of the earth's orbit. The city of Alexandria on the Nile, founded by Alexander, became a center of astonishing discoveries and inventions in the technical, mathematical, and physical domains. Here, Euclid, the founder of Euclidian geometry, taught; here Hero made astonishing technological inventions. Archimedes of Syracuse, an inventor of great war machines and discoverer of natural scientific laws, studied here, and the director of the Library of Alexandria, Eratosthenes (275–195), had already correctly calculated the equator and the spherical shape of the earth. Thus, the doctrine of Copernicus was anticipated in advance. Nonetheless, the Hellenic world was not comprehensive enough for a planetary spatial revolution. Its knowledge remained the concern of the learned, because it had not drawn a world ocean into its existential reality.

When, from Rome outward, Caesar conquered Gaul and England[78] three hundred years later, the Atlantic Ocean was reached and the view to the Northwest was opened. This was the first step toward the contemporary spatial conception of "Europe." In the first century of the Roman imperial period, most strongly indeed at the time of Nero, the consciousness of a deep transformation became so powerful and expansive that one can almost speak of spatial revolutionary transformations, at least with the leading intellects. This historical moment coincides with the first century of our era and thus merits particular attention. The field of vision expanded to the East and to the West, to the North and to the South. Wars of conquest and

78. While Caesar, in books 4 and 5 of his *Commentarii De Bello Gallico*, describes his expeditions to and conquest of Britannia, Schmitt here refers to Britannia as "England" ("England"), thus seeming to refer to Britain and England interchangeably, as he does elsewhere in *Land and Sea* (as in section 9, above; cf. Schmitt [1981], p. 52).

civil wars enveloped space from Spain to Persia, from England to Egypt. Widely distant regions and peoples came into contact with each other and experienced the unity of a common political destiny. From all parts of the Empire, from Germany as from Syria, from Africa or Illyria, a general could be elevated to emperor in Rome by his soldiers. The Isthmus of Corinth was penetrated; Arabia was circumnavigated from the south. Nero sent an expedition to the sources of the Nile. Agrippa's world map and Strabo's *Geography* are documents of this spatial expansion. That the earth has the shape of a sphere was known not only to individual astronomers and mathematicians.

Around this time a famous philosopher, Seneca, teacher and educator and finally a sacrifice to Nero, articulated in grand phrases and verses that which one may already call the planetary feeling of the situation at that time.[79] In all clarity he said that one would need only a not very great number of days from the outermost coast of Spain with some easterly winds, i.e., backwinds, in order to be on the paths westward to reach India lying in the East. In another passage, in the tragedy *Medea*, he announces a remarkable prophecy in beautiful verses:

> The hot Indus and the cold Araxes touch;
> Persians drink from the Elbe and the Rhine.
> Thetis*[80] shall unveil new worlds (novos orbes),
> And Thyïlea shall no longer be the outermost boundary
>   of the earth.[81]

79. In a letter to Ernst Jünger dated April 14, 1940, Schmitt writes: "I've been reading Seneca for awhile. Through all the rhetoric (but then what do we know of this 'rhetoric'?) the dangerous situation is real." Jünger–Schmitt, *Briefe 1930–1983*, p. 92.

80. [Starred note original to Schmitt's German text:] Thetis, the mother of Achilles, stands here as goddess of the sea. In another version "Tiphys" is written; this was the helmsman of the Argo, of the ship on which the Argonauts sailed into the Black Sea, in order to plunder a golden fleece there.

81. Schmitt here appears to quote from Seneca's tragedy *Medea*, ll. 373–79 (omitting lines 375–77), in the edition of Rudolf Peiper and Gustav Richter,

I have cited these verses because they express the comprehensive feeling of space, which was alive in the first century of our era. The beginning of our era was indeed really a pivotal time, which involved not only the consciousness of the fullness of time but also the consciousness of the filled space of the earth and of the planetary horizon. The words of Seneca, however, are secretly connected to modernity and the Age of Discoveries; for they were transmitted across the centuries of spatial obscurity and the terrestrial confinement of the European Middle Ages. The words of Seneca transmitted to thinking humans the feeling of a greater space [*größeren Raumes*] and an expansive world, and even contributed to the discovery of

---

which Carl Schmitt held in his postwar library. Cf. Martin Tielke, "Die Bibliothek Carl Schmitts," Stand: 14.5.2014, Carl-Schmitt-Gesellschaft, p. 420. Carl Schmitt had a 1937 printing of Peiper and Richter's edition of Seneca's tragedies in his library: *L. Annaei Senecae Tragoediae*, rec. Rudolfus Peiper et Gustavus Richter (Bibliotheca scriptorum Graecorum et Romanorum Teubneriana) (Lipsiae, 1937). The quotation from Seneca's *Medea*, ll. 373–79, is spoken by the Chorus of Corinthians (*Chorus Corinthiorum*) and is found on pp. 131–32 of the Peiper and Richter edition. It runs as follows:

> Indus gelidum potat Araxen,
> Albin Persae Rhenumque bibunt.
> venient annis saecula seris,
> quibus Oceanus vincula rerum
> laxet et ingens pateat tellus
> Tethysque novos detegat orbes,
> nec sit terris ultima Thule.

In the passage above, Schmitt seems to omit the three middle lines of the quotation, which might be rendered as follows: "In later years there will come ages, / In which Ocean will loosen its hold on things / and the mighty earth [*tellus*] will open." Seneca, *L. Annaei Senecae Tragoediae*, rec. Rudolfus Peiper et Gustavus Richter, pp. 131–32. That Schmitt was using the edition found in his postwar library is in accord with the previous note (the only note present in the 1942 edition): Peiper and Richter give "Tiphysque" as alternate manuscript reading for "Tethysque" in the apparatus to their edition on the page on which the quote appears. Seneca, *L. Annaei Senecae Tragoediae*, rec. Rudolfus Peiper et Gustavus Richter, p. 132.

America. Christopher Columbus, like many of his contemporaries, knew the words of Seneca and found in them impetus and exhortation for his voyage to the New World, for the bold journey, on which, sailing west, he wished to reach the East, and really reached it. The expression "New World," *novus orbis*, which Seneca used, was promptly applied to the newly discovered America.

The fall of the Roman Empire, the expansion of Islam, the invasions of the Arabs and of the Turks brought about a centuries-long spatial darkening and land confinement in Europe. Being pushed from the sea, the lack of a fleet, [and] the complete confinement to land are markers of the early Middle Ages and its feudal system. In the period from 500 to 1100, Europe became a feudal-agrarian landmass, the ruling class of which, the feudal lords, ceded intellectual and spiritual culture, even reading and writing, to the Church and to the clerisy. Famed rulers and heroes of this period could neither read nor write; for this they had a monk or a chaplain. In a sea empire, the rulers probably could not have remained ignorant of reading and writing for so long as they could in such a purely landbound, agrarian-economic raiment of power. As a result of the Crusades, however, French, English, and German knights and merchants became acquainted with the Near East. In the North, the expansion of the German Hanseatic League[82] and the Teutonic Knights[83] opened a new horizon; here a system of

---

82. In Schmitt's original German text, "German" is capitalized in both "German Hanseatic League" and "German [Teutonic] Knights" ("der Deutschen Hanse und der Deutsche Ritterorden"), which, at least in the first instance, it need not be according to standard German grammar. "German" in "German Hanseatic League" appears to be capitalized for emphasis.

83. The Teutonic Knights (*Deutsche Ritterorden*) were a monastic order that launched campaigns for Christianization and German imperial expansion in Lithuania, Poland, Estonia, and the Baltic on behalf of the Holy Roman Empire in the thirteenth, fourteenth, and fifteenth centuries. The insignia of

traffic and trade emerged, which came to be called the "World economy of the Middle Ages."[84]

In addition, this spatial expansion was simultaneously a cultural transformation of a thoroughgoing kind. Everywhere in Europe new forms of political life emerged. In France, England, and Sicily centralized administrations were created that in many ways anticipate the modern state. In northern and central Italy, a new city culture grew. Universities developed with a new theological science and a heretofore unknown juristic science, and the rebirth of Roman law created a new educated class, the jurists, which broke the educational monopoly of the Church clerisy, which was typical for the medieval feudal period. In the new, Gothic art, in architecture, in sculpture, and in painting, a powerful rhythm of movement overcomes the static space in the Romanesque art, which preceded it, and puts in its place a dynamic force field, a space of movement. The Gothic arch is a structure in which the parts and pieces mutually bear one another up and hold one another in equipoise through their weight. Set against the stable, heavy masses of Romanesque building, this is a fully new feeling of space. But also in comparison with the space of the ancient temple and the space of the architecture of the Renaissance that follows it, Gothic art reveals an expression of a unique, space-transforming force and movement.

---

the order of the Teutonic Knights was a black cross on a white field. The translator is grateful to Pierre-Yves Modicom for this reference.

84. Schmitt here may refer to Fritz Rörig's *Mittelalterliche Weltwirtschaft: Blüte und Ende einer Weltwirtschaftsperiode* (Jena: G. Fischer, 1933). In his postwar library, Schmitt held four books by Rörig, and in 1941 Schmitt cited Rörig in "Staatliche Souveränität und freies Meer," one of the articles in which he prepared an earlier version of the arguments of *Land and Sea*. Cf. Tielke, "Die Bibliothek Carl Schmitts," pp. 363–64; Carl Schmitt, "Staatliche Souveränität und freies Meer: Über den Gegensatz von Land und See im Völkerrecht der Neuzeit," pp. 400–30, in *Staat, Großraum, Nomos*, p. 416n14.

## 12

Further historical examples could be found, but all pale before the deepest and most consequential alteration in the whole of world history known to us. It falls in the sixteenth and seventeenth centuries, in the epoch of the discovery of America and of the first circumnavigation of the earth. Now a new world emerges, in the bravest sense of the term, and the collective consciousness, first, of the western and central European peoples, and then, finally, the whole of human collective consciousness is transformed from the ground up. This is the first authentic spatial revolution in the full, earth- and world-encompassing sense of the term.

It is comparable to no other. It was not somehow only a particularly comprehensive quantitative spatial expansion of the geographic horizon, which entered of its own accord as a result of the discovery of new parts of the earth and new seas. Rather, for human collective consciousness the whole picture of our planet and, beyond this, the whole astronomical conception of the entire universe were changed, with the complete abandonment of received ancient and medieval conceptions. For the first time in its history, the human held the whole terrestrial orb like a ball in its hand. That the earth should be a sphere appeared to a medieval human, but also still appeared to Martin Luther, as a ridiculous fantasy, not to be taken seriously. Now, the spherical shape of the earth became a comprehensible fact, an irrefutable experience, and an indisputable scientific truth. Now, the earth, until then so fixed, moved around the sun. But even this was not yet the deepest actual spatial alteration that, from now on, entered. The expansion of the cosmos and the conception of an infinite, empty space were decisive.

Copernicus was the first to show scientifically that the earth revolves around the sun. His work on the revolutions of the heavenly spheres, *De revolutionibus orbium coelestium*,[85] appeared in 1543. With it, indeed, Copernicus changed our star system, however, he still held fast to the notion that the universe in its entirety, the cosmos, is a bounded space. The world in the grand cosmic sense and, with it, the concept of space itself had thus not yet been altered. A few decades later the boundaries fell. In the philosophic system of Giordano Bruno, the star system, in which the earth moves around the sun as a planet, is only one of many star systems in the infinite celestial firmament. As a consequence of Galileo's scientific experiments, such philosophic speculations became a mathematically demonstrable truth. Kepler calculated the orbits of the planets, although it made even him shudder when he conceived the infinity of such spaces, in which the systems of planets moved without conceivable boundaries and without a center. With Newton's theory, the new conception of space was established for the whole of enlightened Europe. Planets, masses, and matter moved, with forces of attraction and repulsion balancing each other according to the laws of gravity in an infinite, empty space.

Humans could thus now conceive of an empty space, which they could not have previously done, even if some philosophers might have wished to speak of "emptiness." Previously, humans feared emptiness; they had the so-called *horror vacui*.[86] Now they forget their fear and are not at all worried by the fact that they and their world exist in a vacuum. The writers of the Enlightenment, with Voltaire at the forefront, even felt very proud of such a scientifically demonstrable conception of a world in an infinite empty space. But attempt just once to really conceive for yourself a really empty space! Not only a space emptied of air

---

85. Schmitt gives the title of Copernicus's book in Latin in quotation marks in the German original, preceded by a vernacular translation of the title.

86. "Horror vacui" ("fear of the vacuum" or "fear of the empty") is Latin and italicized in Schmitt's original German.

but rather a space wholly empty of even the most sublime and refined matter! Attempt just once in your imagination to really distinguish space and matter, to separate both from each other and think to yourself the one without the other! You can just as well think the absolute Nothing. The *lumières*[87] laughed much about this *horror vacui*. But this was perhaps only the graspable shudder before the Nothing and before the emptiness of death, before a nihilistic conception and before Nihilism itself.

Such a change, like the one contained in the thought of an infinite, empty space, cannot simply be explained as the consequence of a mere geographical expansion of the known earth. It is so fundamental and revolutionary that one can equally well say, inversely, that the discovery of new continents and the circumnavigation of the earth are only the manifestations and consequences of transformations that lie deeper. Only on this account could landing on an unknown island inaugurate an entire Age of Discoveries. Humans often landed in America from the west or from the east. As is well known, the Vikings already found America from Greenland around the year 1000, and the Indians, whom Columbus found there already, also had to come to America from somewhere. But, nonetheless, America was first "discovered" in 1492 by Columbus. The "pre-Columbian" discoveries affected neither a planetary spatial revolution nor did they take place in the course of such a revolution. If they had, the Aztecs would not have stayed in Mexico and the Incas would not have stayed in Peru; one day, with a map of the earth in hand, they would have paid us a visit in Europe and, instead of us discovering them, they would have discovered us. There is more to a spatial revolution than landing in a heretofore unknown place. A spatial revolution involves a change in the concepts of space encompassing all the levels and domains of human existence. The enormous temporal

---

87. Alt: "the people of the Enlightenment" (*Aufklärer*).

turn of the sixteenth and seventeenth centuries evinces what this means.

In these centuries of a temporal turn, European humanity simultaneously imposed upon all the domains of its creative spirit a new concept of space. The painting of the Renaissance laid aside the space of medieval Gothic painting; the painters now painted humans and things placed in a space, which perspectivally generates an empty depth. Humans and things now stand and move *within* a space.[88] In comparison with the space of a Gothic image, this signifies, in fact, another world. That the painters now see otherwise, that their eye is altered, is, for us, very meaningful. Indeed, the great painters are not somehow only persons who fool one with something beautiful. Art is a historical index of spatial consciousness, and the real painter is a human, who sees humans and things better and more correctly than other humans, more correctly in the sense of the historical reality of his own time. But not only in painting does a new space emerge.[89] The architecture of the Renaissance creates for itself its classical geometrically partitioned buildings, differentiated from Gothic space by a worldwide expanse; the sculpture of the Renaissance poses the statues of human figures free in space, while medieval figures are "angled" upon pillars and walls. Baroque architecture, by contrast, presses in a dynamic movement and thereby stands in some relation with Gothic architecture, but it nonetheless remains firmly trapped in the new, modern space that emerged through the spatial revolution and which it decisively worked to create. Music extracts its mel-

88. The italics of the single word are present and italicize the corresponding term in Schmitt's German text ("Die Menschen und Dinge stehen und bewegen sich jetzt *in* einem Raum.").

89. In the 1942 and 1954 editions, this sentence reads: "But not only in the painting of the Renaissance (*der Renaissance*) does a new space emerge." In the 1981 edition, the phrase "of the Renaissance" (*der Renaissance*) was omitted. Schmitt (1942), p. 48; Schmitt (1954), p. 40; Schmitt (1981), p. 69.

odies and harmonies out of the old keys and places them in the auditory space of our so-called tonal system. Theater and opera allow their figures to move in the empty depths of a scenic space on stage, which is separated from the space of the spectators by a curtain. All these intellectual currents from both of these centuries, the Renaissance, Humanism, the Reformation, the Counter-Reformation, and Baroque, thus contributed to the totality of this spatial revolution.

It is no overstatement to claim that all domains of life, all forms of existence, all kinds of human creative force, art, science, and technology partake in the new concept of space. The great changes in the geographic picture of the earth are now only a foregrounded aspect of the deep transformation, which is implied in a term as consequential as "spatial revolution." That which is called the rational superiority of the European, that which has been termed the European spirit and "Occidental rationalism," now advances irresistibly. It develops in the western and central European peoples, destroys the medieval forms of human community, builds new states, fleets, and armies, invents new machines, subjugates the non-European peoples, and places them before the dilemma of either adopting European civilization or of descending to the status of a mere colonial people.

## 13

Every fundamental order is a spatial order. One speaks of the constitution of a country or a piece of earth as of its fundamental order, its Nomos.*[90] Now, the true, actual fundamental order

90. [Starred note to Schmitt's original German 1981 text, added to the 1954 edition and retained in the 1981 edition:] The Greek noun *Nomos* comes from the Greek verb *Nemein* and like this it has three meanings. *Nemein* is, in the first instance, the same as: to take, to appropriate (Nehmen). Consequently *Nomos* means in the first instance: appropriation (die Nahme). As in Greek, e.g., *Legein-Logos* is parallel to the German for to speak/speech [language] (Sprechen-Sprache), similarly the Greek: *Nemein-Nomos* is parallel to

touches in its essential core upon particular spatial boundaries and separations, upon particular quantities and a particular partition of the earth. At the beginning of every great epoch there stands a great land-appropriation. In particular, every significant alteration and every resituating of the image of the earth is bound up with world-political alterations and with a new division of the earth, with a new land-appropriation.

Such an astounding, unexampled spatial revolution, like that of the sixteenth and seventeenth centuries, must lead to an equally astounding, unexampled land-appropriation. The European peoples to whom the new, apparently infinite spaces opened and who swarmed out into these expansive spaces, treated the non-European and non-Christian lands and peoples that they discovered like ownerless property, belonging to the first Europeans who took it in possession. In doing this, all conquerors, Catholic as well as Protestant, invoked their mission to spread Christianity to non-Christian peoples. One could have attempted this without conquest and plundering. However, no other rationalization and justification was given.

---

the German for to appropriate/appropriation (Nehmen-Nahme). Appropriation is in the first instance land-appropriation, later sea-appropriation as well, of which much has been said in our world-historical meditation, and in the domain of industry, industrial appropriation, i.e., seizing the industrial means of production. Second, *Nemein* means: partition and distribution [*Teilen und Verteilen*] of that which has been taken. *Nomos* is thus second: the fundamental partition and distribution of the soil and the order of property which touches upon it. The third meaning is: to pasture (*Weiden*), i.e., using, economizing, and valuing of the soil derived from its partition, production, and consumption. Appropriating-Partitioning-Pasturing (*Nehmen-Teilen-Weiden*) are, in this sequence, the three fundamental concepts of any concrete order. Further on the meaning of *Nomos* in the book: *The Nomos of the Earth* (Cologne, 1950). (Second Edition, Berlin, 1974). [Translator's note: This note by Schmitt is wholly absent from the 1942 edition of *Land and Sea*. In this note, one of two notes to Schmitt's 1981 text, the reference to the second edition of *The Nomos of the Earth* is absent from the 1954 edition of *Land and Sea*. Cf. Schmitt (1954), p. 41n; Schmitt (1942), pp. 49–50.]

Some monks, e.g., the Spanish theologian Francisco de Vitoria in his lectures on the Indians (*De Indis*, 1532),[91] claimed that the right of peoples [*Recht der Völker*][92] to their soil is independent of their religious faith, and he defended the rights of the Indians in an astoundingly courageous way. This changes nothing in the overall historical picture of the European land-appropriation. Later, in the eighteenth and nineteenth centuries, the mandate of the Christian missionaries becomes the mandate to spread European civilization to non-civilized peoples. From such justifications a Christian-European law of peoples [*Völkerrecht*][93] emerged, i.e., a community of the Christian

91. Schmitt here refers to the theologian Francisco de Vitoria's (ca. 1483–1546) lectures *De Indis insulanis relectio prior* and *De Indis, sive de iure belli Hispanorum in barbaros, Relectio posterior*, both printed in Vitoria's posthumously published *Relectiones theologicae XII. in duos tomos divisae*, 2 vols. (Lugduni: apud Iacobum Boyerium, 1557), vol. 1, pp. 282–374, 375–425. In the 1942 edition, the title of the work is given as "De Jndis," while in the 1954 and 1981 editions the title is given as "De Indis." Cf. Schmitt (1942), p. 50; Schmitt (1954), p. 42; Schmitt (1981), p. 72.

92. Schmitt's use of *Recht der Völker*, translated as "right of peoples," is an inversion of the more standard term for the law of peoples, *Völkerrecht*. The latter term emphasizes legal relations between different nations, or peoples, while the former, Schmitt's formulation, focuses on the integrity of a people's claim to its territory.

93. Here and throughout, *Völkerrecht* has been rendered as "law of peoples," consistent with Schmitt's understanding of *Völkerrecht* as the appropriate term to render the Roman legal tradition of *ius gentium*. Cf. Schmitt, *Völkerrechtliche Großraumordnung mit Interventionsverbot für raumfremde Mächte, Ein Beitrag zum Reichsbegriff im Völkerrecht* (Dritte, unveränderte Auflage der Ausgabe von 1941) (Berlin: Duncker & Humblot, 2009 [1941]), p. 11: "Völkerrecht als *jus gentium*, als ein Recht der Völker, zunächst eine *personal*, d.h. von der Volks- und Staatsangehörigkeit her bestimmte, konkrete Ordnung." While G. L. Ulmen in his important translation of Schmitt's *Der Nomos der Erde* (1950/1974) chose to translate *Völkerrecht* as "international law," in the 1940s, when Schmitt was writing *Land und Meer*, Schmitt explicitly contrasted *Völkerrecht*, which associated with his notion of a *Völkerrechtliche Großraumordnung*, with the term "international law" (deploying the term in quotation marks in English in the German original) or, in Schmitt's terms, "das sogenannte internationales Recht." Cf. Carl

peoples of Europe spreading over the entirety of the remaining world. This constructed a "family of nations," an inter-state order. Its law of peoples was based on the distinction between the Christian and the non-Christian, or, a century later, between civilized and non-civilized peoples (in the Christian-European sense). A people that was not civilized in this sense could not be a member of this community of the law of peoples; it was not a subject but, rather, only an object of this law of peoples, i.e., it

---

Schmitt, "Die Auflösung der europäischen Ordnung im 'International Law' (1890–1939)," in *Deutsche Rechtwissenschaft* 5:4 (1940), pp. 267–78; reprinted in *Staat, Großraum, Nomos*, pp. 372–87, at p. 372. As he does in section 10 of *Land and Sea* (and in the prologue to his postwar *Gespräch über den Neuen Raum* [1955/1958]), Schmitt often uses the terms *Großraum* and *Lebensraum* seemingly interchangeably and understands German expansion into German-speaking territories to be consistent with his notion of a *Völkerrechtliche Großraumordnung* even if "international law" may be cited to the contrary. Cf. Schmitt, *Völkerrechtliche Großraumordnung*, pp. 23, 35, 46–48. While Schmitt does view a system of "international law" as a universalistic expansion of *Völkerrecht*, or the law of peoples, he associates the former notion with the "Geneva League of Nations" and the Treaty of Versailles, which Schmitt called the "Parisian Suburb Treaty" (*Pariser Vorortvertrag*), and he associates the latter notion, *Völkerrecht*, with the *Jus Publicum Europaeum*, concerning only European states and European peoples. Cf. Schmitt, "Die Auflösung der europäischen Ordnung im 'International Law' (1890–1939)," p. 372; Schmitt, *Völkerrechtliche Großraumordnung*, p. 15. In *Land and Sea*, Schmitt claims that the root distinction of the *Jus Publicum Europaeum* (and thus, of his notion of *Völkerrecht*) concerns Christian European peoples (*Völker*) and does not apply to non-Christian peoples (thereby excluding Jews from rights under the law of peoples) and also does not apply to non-European peoples (the English turn away from the continent thus deprives England of rights under the law of peoples in its war with Germany, in Schmitt's view). In this sense, sections 10 through 13 of *Land and Sea* fit with the anti-Jewish passages of the work (sections 3, 17, and 18), and these sections constitute a single unified argument. England's turn to the sea, in Schmitt's presentation, also fits with this argument—under the law of peoples, under *Völkerrecht* as Schmitt understands this term, neither Jews nor the English have rights against Germany in World War II, according to Schmitt, whatever "international law" may say to the contrary.

belonged among the possessions of one of the civilized peoples as a colony or as a colonial protectorate.

You should not conceive of this "community of the Christian-European peoples" as a flock of peaceful lambs. They conducted bloody wars among themselves. However, this does not abolish the historical fact of a Christian-European-civilized community and order. World history is a history of land-appropriations, and with every land-appropriation, the land-appropriators not only contracted with each other but they also often fought, often even in bloody wars between brothers. Nonetheless, the land-appropriators had, among themselves, in contrast with the old possessors and foreign third parties, one thing in common. Internal wars, wars between brothers, and civil wars are acknowledged to be the most cruel of all wars. This holds, above all, for common land-appropriations. And wars are all the more intense the more valuable the object of battle. Here, the war was concerned with the land-appropriation of a new world. In the sixteenth century, e.g., in Florida, the Spanish and the French massacred each other for years in the most gruesome manner and spared neither women nor children. The Spanish and the English conducted one hundred years of bitter war against each other, in which the brutal enmity of which humans are capable appeared to reach its highest degree of intensity. In addition, the deployment of non-Europeans, Mohammedans,[94] or Indians as overt or covert aids or even as allies was never a cause of concern. The outbreaks of enmity were terrible; people called one another murderers, thieves, rapists, and pirates. Only a single accusation was absent, which was, however, directed especially against Indians: among Christian Europeans one did not accuse another of cannibalism. Otherwise, nothing was lacking in the vocabulary of embittered, deadly enmity. And yet

---

94. "Mohammedans" here translates Schmitt's "Mohammedaner." Schmitt (1981), p. 74; cf. section 4, above.

this disappears in the face of the all-ruling fact of a common European land-appropriation of the New World. The sense and core of the Christian-European law of peoples, its fundamental order, lay in the partition of the new earth. Among themselves the European peoples were, without much planned reflection, united in treating the non-European soil of the earth as colonial soil, i.e., as an object for their conquest and exploitation. This side of historical development is so important that one can equally well, and perhaps more rightly, call the Age of Discoveries the Age of European land-appropriation. War, Heraclitus says, brings together, and the law is strife.[95]

## 14

The Portuguese, the Spanish, the French, the Dutch, and the English fought among themselves over the partition of the new earth. The battle was not only conducted with military weapons; it was also a diplomatic and juristic conflict over the

95. Schmitt here apparently refers to what is Heraclitus fragment 22 B 80 in Diels-Kranz, *Die Fragmente der Vorsokratiker, Griechisch und Deutsch*, 10th ed. (Berlin: Weidmann, 1961), taken from Celsus VI.xlii. In the vernacular translation in Diels-Kranz, fragment B 80 reads as follows: "Man muß wissen, daß der Krieg Gemeinsames ist und daß Recht Streit ist/und daß alles geschieht in Übereinstimmung mit Streit und so auch gebraucht wird" ("One must know that war is common and that law is strife/and that everything occurs in accord with strife and is also thus deployed"). Jacob Taubes would refer to this Heraclitus fragment in requesting the title for his posthumously published collection of texts related to Schmitt. Jacob Taubes, *Ad Carl Schmitt: Gegenstrebige Fügung* (Berlin: Merve Verlag, 1987), pp. 79–80. Cf. Carl Schmitt, *Terra e Mare: Una riflessione sulla storia del mondo*, trans. Giovanni Gurisatti (Milan: Adelphi Edizioni, 2011 [2002]), p. 77n1. Schmitt had a postwar edition of *Die Fragmente der Vorsokratiker* in his postwar library: "Diels, Hermann: Die Fragmente der Vorsokratiker. Mit Einführungen u. Bibliographien von Gert Plamböck. Nach d. von Walther Kranz hrsg., 8. Aufl. (Rowohlts Klassiker der Literatur und der Wissenschaft, 10), Hamburg 1957." Martin Tielke, "Die Bibliothek Carl Schmitts (Monographien)," p. 91; cf. Jaap Mansfeld and Primavesi Oliver, eds., *Die Vorsokratiker, Griechisch und Deutsch* (Stuttgart: Reclam, 2012 [2011]), pp. 264–65.

better legal title. Against the indigenous one could, in any case, be quite generous in this regard. One landed, erected a cross or inscribed the King's flag in a tree, set up a moveable flagstone, or laid an announcement in the hole of a tree stump. The Spanish loved announcing in festive proclamations passing by a harbor of indigenous people that this land from now on belonged to the Crown of Castile. Such symbolic seizures of possession were held sufficient to legally acquire great islands and whole continents. No government, neither the Portuguese, nor the Spanish, nor the Dutch, nor the English, respected the rights of the native-born and indigenous population to their own soil. The conflict of the European land-appropriating peoples among themselves was another question. Here, everyone invoked every legal claim available to them, and, when it seemed expedient, this included treaties with the indigenous peoples and their princes.

As long as Portugal and Spain, two Catholic powers, were alone among themselves, the Pope in Rome could intervene as the creator of legal titles, as the order ordaining new land-appropriations, and as claims judge between the two land-appropriating powers. In the year 1493, thus hardly a year after the discovery of America, the Spanish had already obtained an edict from Alexander VI, who was then Pope, in which the Pope, by force of his apostolic authority, gifted the newly discovered West Indian lands to the King of Castile and Leon and his heirs as a worldly fiefdom of the Church. In the edict, a line was drawn running through the Atlantic Ocean, 100 miles west of the Azores and Cape Verde. All discoveries west of the line were granted by the Pope to Spain as a fiefdom. In the following years, Spain and Portugal came to an agreement in the Treaty of Tordesillas that all land discovered east of the line should belong to Portugal. Thus, the partition of the whole New World begins immediately in the grandest style, although, at that time,

Columbus had only just discovered a few islands and coastal promontories. No one at this time could make a correct image of the earth, but the new partition of the earth set in nonetheless in full scope and in every form. The papal line of partition from 1493 stands at the beginning of the battle for the new fundamental order, for the new *nomos* of the earth.

For over a hundred years, the Spanish and Portuguese invoked the papal grants in order to fend off the claims of the advancing French, Dutch, and English. Brazil, discovered by Cabral in 1500, became Portuguese without contradiction because this piece of land jutting out from the western coast[96] of America fell in the eastern, Portuguese half of the earth due to a later relocation of the line of partition toward the west. But the other land-appropriating powers did not feel themselves bound by the accords between the Spanish and the Portuguese, and papal authority was not sufficient to infuse them with respect for the monopoly on land-appropriation held by both the Catholic powers. Then, through the Reformation, the peoples who became Protestant openly withdrew from any authority of the Roman Pope. Thus the battle for the land-appropriation of the new earth became a battle between the Reformation and the Counter-Reformation, between the World Catholicism of the Spanish and the World Protestantism of the Huguenots, the Dutch, and the English.

## 15

Over and against the indigenous populations of the newly discovered lands, the Christian land-appropriators made no common front, because there was no common opponent capable

---

96. One normally refers to Brazil as located on the east coast of South Africa, but Schmitt refers to "the western coast" because he is thinking from the perspective of the ocean, not the continent.

of battle. All the more arduous, but also all the grander historically and all the more formative, was the War of Religion now setting in between the land-appropriating Christian peoples, the world battle between Protestantism and Catholicism. With this characterization and with these fronts, it manifested itself as a War of Religion, and this it was indeed. But, with this, all has not been said. It first receives its true and full light when we here heed the opposition of the elements and the separation between the world of the free sea and the world of the solid land, which was beginning at that time.

Some figures from the great religious battle were set upon the stage by the great poets. The Spanish King Philip II and his enemy, the English Queen Elizabeth, became a favorite theme of dramatists. Both appear in different dramas by Schiller, both are also often treated in immediate juxtaposition within the same play. This yields beautiful and effective scenes upon the stage. But the deepest oppositions, the actual friend–enemy situations, and the last elementary forces and oppositions cannot be made visible in this way. In Germany in the same period there are no comparably heroic figures fit for the stage. Out of these years from 1550 to 1618, so poor in deeds for Germany, only a lone German became the hero of a significant tragic drama: the Emperor Rudolf II. You will have heard little of him, and one really cannot say that he lives on in the historical memory of the German people. But for all this, his name still belongs in this connection, and a great German dramatist, Franz Grillparzer, rightly places him in the middle of a tragedy: *A Brother's Dispute in Hapsburg* [*Ein Bruderzwist in Habsburg*].[97] The problem and grandeur of the Grillparzerian

---

97. A 1941 edition of Franz Grillparzer's 1848 drama *Ein Bruderzwist in Habsburg* was present in Schmitt's postwar library. Cf. Tielke, "Die Bibliothek Carl Schmitts," Stand: 14.5.2014, p. 147: "Grillparzer, Franz: Ein Bruderzwist in Habsburg. Trauerspiel in 5 Aufz. (Insel-Bücherei, 417 [a]), Leipzig 1941."

play, like that of its hero, lie precisely in the fact that Rudolf II was not an active hero but, rather, that he was an upholder, a delayer. He had something of a "Katechon," a concept that we have already once mentioned in another connection (p. 17). What could Rudolf even do in the situation of Germany at that time? It was already quite a lot when he recognized that the fronts beyond Germany didn't concern Germany, and it was already an achievement when he really held up and postponed the outbreak of the Thirty Years' War by decades.

The peculiarity of the situation of Germany at that time consisted, indeed, in the fact that Germany had not made a decision in this war of religion, nor was it even capable of doing so. It bore the opposition between Protestantism and Catholicism in itself, but this opposition internal to Germany was something wholly other than the world-encompassing world opposition between Catholicism and Protestantism, which related to the land-appropriation of the new earth. Germany was indeed the home of Luther and the land in which the Reformation originated. But the battle of the world-appropriating powers had long outstripped the initial opposition between Catholicism and Protestantism and, far beyond the questions internal to Germany, had attained the much deeper and more precise opposition between Jesuitism and Calvinism.[98] This was now the dominant world-political friend–enemy distinction.

The German Lutheran princes and orders, above all the first Protestant prince of the Empire, the Elector of Saxony, strove to demonstrate their loyalty even to a Catholic Emperor. When, due to Calvinistic pressure, a military alliance of the

---

Schmitt makes reference to this play in a letter to Ernst Rudolf Huber dated August 21, 1942. Carl Schmitt–Ernst Rudolf Huber, *Briefwechsel 1926–1981, Mit ergänzenden Materialien*, ed. Ewald Grothe (Berlin: Duncker & Humblot, 2014), p. 302 and 302n1342.

98. "Jesuitism" here translates Schmitt's "Jesuitismus."

German Protestant orders, the so-called Union, emerged, and the Catholic orders constructed a counter-front, the so-called *Liga*,[99] the Lutheran Elector of Saxony did not know where he belonged. Even in 1612 there were negotiations concerning his admission to the Catholic *Liga*. The hatred of the Lutherans against the Calvinists was no less than their hatred against the Papists,[100] also no less than the hatred of the Catholics against the Calvinists. This is not only to be explained on the ground that the Lutherans, in general practice, hold more to the basic principle of submitting to the powers that be[101] than do the much more activist Calvinists. The real reason lies in the fact that Germany at that time had been excluded from the European land-appropriation of the New World and was dragged into the world conflict between the land-appropriating western European powers from the outside. Simultaneously, it was threatened in the southeast by the encroaching Turks.[102] Jesuits and Calvinists from Spain, Holland, and England confronted Germany with alternatives that were thoroughly alien to the internal development of Germany. Non-Jesuit Catholic princes and orders and non-Calvinist German Lutheran princes and orders sought to avoid the conflict, which was essentially foreign to them. But, for this, a powerful force and resoluteness of their own would have been needed. For lack of such, they fell into a situation that one has fittingly described

99. Schmitt deploys the Italian term for "league" in his German original, in which the term is not italicized. While the term "Liga" is absent from Grimms *Wörterbuch*, the term "Katholische Liga" was standard usage in German historical scholarship of the 1940s to refer to the Catholic League. The translator is thankful to Lars Vinx for this reference.

100. "Papists" here translates Schmitt's "Papisten."

101. Cf. Romans 13:1–4.

102. Here, and throughout section 15, Schmitt refers to the Empire of the Austrian Habsburgs as part of Germany ("Deutschland"). Earlier in this section, Schmitt had referred to Franz Grillparzer, an Austrian playwright, as a German writer.

as "neutral-passive."[103] The consequence was that Germany became the battlefield of an overseas war of land-appropriation internally foreign to itself, without itself partaking in the land-appropriation. Calvinism was the new fighting religion;[104] Calvinism was grasped by the elementary rupture upon the sea as the faith suited to it. It became the faith of French Huguenots, of Dutch heroes of liberty, and of English Puritans. It was also the religious persuasion of the Great Elector of Brandenburg, one of the few German princes who had a sense for sea-power and colonies. The inland Calvinist communities in Switzerland, in Hungary, and in other lands were, viewed world-politically, without significance if they did not stand in the wake of these maritime energies.[105]

103. Here, Schmitt may refer to a passage in a collection of historical materials related to the Thirty Years' War, Anton Chroust's twelve-volume *Briefe und Akten zur Geschichte des Dreissigjährigen Krieges in den Zeiten des Vorwaltenden Einflusses der Wittelsbacher*. In a note to the tenth volume of the collection, one reads: "Da Brömser den Modus voriger Verhandlungen angreift, so erinnert Khlesl, dass der Prager Konvent im Jahr 1610 den früheren Akkord von 1608 bestätigt und dabei Brömser selber mitgewirkt habe; auch den neuen Vergleich von 1611 hätten die Kurfürsten in Nürnberg sich gefallen lassen; die Krönung habe sich aus der Vergleichung des Kaisers und der Stände bei offenem Landtage ergeben; der König habe sich dabei 'neutro-passiv' verhalten und sich der Kurfürsten Intervention nicht misfallen lassen; niemand, der damals an Ort und Stelle war und die Umstände kannte, hätte anders raten und schliessen können." Anton Chroust, ed., *Briefe und Akten zur Geschichte des Dreissigjährigen Krieges in den Zeiten des Vorwaltenden Einflusses der Wittelsbacher*, 12 vols. (Munich: M. Riegersche Universitäts-Buchhandlung, 1906), vol. 10, p. 127n2.

104. In the 1942 edition, this sentence ends with a period after "religion." Schmitt (1942), p. 58. In the 1954 and 1981 editions, the period is replaced by a semicolon joining what had been two sentences in the 1942 edition. In the 1942 and 1954 editions, "religion" ("Religion") has a standard spelling, but has been printed as "Relegion" in the 1981 edition (and successor editions). The editors read "Relegion" as a typographic error for "Religion" in the 1981 edition (and successor editions). Cf. Schmitt (1942), p. 58; Schmitt (1954), p. 48; Schmitt (1981), p. 82.

105. In the 1981 edition (and successor editions), a paragraph break was introduced following this sentence. This break was not present in the 1942

All non-Calvinists were shocked by the Calvinistic faith, above all by the hard faith in the pre-selection of humans since eternity, in "predestination." In a worldly sense, the faith in predestination is only the most extreme heightening of the consciousness of belonging to a world different from that corrupt world which is damned to downfall. It is, in the parlance of modern sociology, the highest degree of the self-consciousness of an elite, which is certain of its rank and of its historical hour. More simply, more humanly spoken, it is the certainty of being saved, and salvation is now, once and for all, the decisive sense, counter to any other notion,[106] of all world history. In this certainty, the Dutch Beggars[107] sang their glorious song: "The land shall be sea, thus it shall be free."

When the elementary energies of the sea were unleashed in the sixteenth century, their success was so great that they quickly entered into the domain of political world history. At this moment, they also had to enter into the spiritual language of their time. They could not remain mere whale-hunters, sailors, and sea dogs. They had to seek their spiritual allies, the boldest and most radical allies, the ones who most thoroughly

---

and 1954 editions, in which this paragraph and the following formed a single, continuous paragraph.

106. Schmitt's phrase "der gegen jeden Begriff entscheidende Sinn" here may also carry the connotation of "the decisive sense, independent of any [conceptual] label."

107. Of the so-called "Beggars," active in the Dutch Revolt against Spanish imperial rule in the Low Countries in the sixteenth and seventeenth centuries, Martin van Gelderen writes: "A dramatic turn of events occurred on 1 April 1572. A fleet of Sea Beggars, ordered by Queen Elizabeth to leave the English harbours, was driven by a storm to the coast of Holland and Zeeland, and more or less by coincidence, they captured the town of Brill in Holland. The Sea Beggars, often acting like pirates, more or less formed the naval forces of the rebels in exile." Martin van Gelderen, *The Political Thought of the Dutch Revolt, 1555–1590* (Cambridge: Cambridge Univ. Press, 1992), pp. 41–42. In the context of the Dutch Revolt, "Beggars" could refer both to those "Sea Beggars" who made up the Dutch navy in exile as well as to the members of the Dutch resistance more generally. Cf. ibid., pp. 104, 61n102.

put an end to the images of the earlier age. This could not be the German Lutheranism of that time. German Lutheranism rather involved a tendency toward territorialism and a general confinement to the land. In any case, in Germany, the end of the Hanseatic League and German power in the Baltic Sea fall as significantly into the Lutheran period as the maritime ascent of Holland and Cromwell's violent decision coincide with the Calvinistic period. Of all things, this has only barely entered our consciousness. Most historical investigations up until now remain under land-oriented perspectives. They have before their eyes only solid land and state development, in Germany, even only territorial-state development, and are often in addition still wholly concerned with small states and small spaces. However, if we turn our gaze toward the sea, then we immediately see the confluence or, if I may so express myself, the world-historical fraternity that combines political Calvinism with the upswelling maritime energies of Europe. The religious fronts and the theological battle parlance of this period also carry in their core the opposition between elementary forces that effected a re-positioning of world-historical existence from solid land to the sea.

## 16

While on the land side of historical events a land-appropriation proceeded in the grandest style, at sea the other, no less important half of the new partition of our planet was completed. This occurred through the British appropriation of the sea. On the sea side, this is the event of the complete European rupture during these centuries. Through it, the baseline of the first planetary spatial revolution was defined, the essence of which lies in the separation between land and sea. The firm land now belongs to a dozen sovereign states, the sea belongs to no one or to all or finally only to one: England. The order of the firm land consists in its division into state dominions; the high sea is free, i.e., state-free and subject to the authority of no state dominion. These are the basic spatial facts, out of which the Christian-European law of peoples developed in the last three hundred years. This was[108] the basic law, the *nomos* of the earth in this epoch.

Only in light of this originary deed of the British appropriation of the sea and the division of land and sea do many famous and oft-cited sentences and slogans receive their true sense. Thus, the expression of Walter Raleigh: "Whoever rules the sea rules world trade, and whoever rules world trade owns all the treasures of the world and, indeed, the world itself."[109] Or: "All trade is world trade; all world trade is sea trade." To this, at the height of English sea power and English world power, there is appended the slogan of freedom: "All world trade is free trade." All this is not simply false, but it is bound to a particular time and a particular world situation, and it becomes

108. In the 1942 edition of Schmitt's text, this sentence reads: "This *is* the basic law, the nomos of the earth in this epoch" (emphasis added). In the 1954 edition, Schmitt altered this sentence by changing "is" (*ist*) to "was" (*war*), an alteration retained in the 1981 edition. Cf. Schmitt (1942), p. 60; Schmitt (1954), p. 50; Schmitt (1981), p. 86. In his *Dialogue on New Space* (*Gespräch über den neuen Raum* [1955/1958]), composed in the year after Schmitt published the revised, 1954 edition of *Land and Sea*, Schmitt claims that atomic and hydrogen power obviated the spatial order of land and sea.

109. Here, Schmitt may refer to Walter Raleigh's "A Discourse of the Invention of Ships, Anchors, Compass, &c." In this text, Raleigh writes, "As *Popelinire* well observeth, the Forces of Princes by Sea are *Marques de Grandeur d'Estat*, are Marks of the Greatness of an Estate: For whosoever commands the Sea, commands the Trade; whosoever commands the Trade of the World, commands the Riches of the World, and consequently the World itself." Walter Raleigh, *The Works of Sir Walter Ralegh, Kt.: Political, Commercial, and Philosophical; Together with his Letters and Poems. The whole never before collected together, and some never yet printed. To which is prefix'd, a new account of his life by Tho. Birch*, 2 vols. (London: R. Dodsley, 1751), vol. 2, pp. 79–80. Raleigh's "A Discourse of the Invention of Ships, Anchors, Compass, &c." was also reprinted in numerous nineteenth-century editions of Raleigh's collected works.

false if one seeks to make absolute and eternal truths out of it. Above all, the cleft between land and sea unveils itself in the cleft between land war and sea war. Land war and sea war were indeed always different things strategically and tactically. Now, however, their opposition becomes an expression of different worlds and opposed legal persuasions.

For land war, the states of the European continent have constructed certain forms since the sixteenth century, at the basis of which lies the thought that war is a relation between state and state. On both sides there is state-organized military power, and the armies carry out battle among one another on the open battlefield. Only the fighting hosts confront one another as enemies, while the non-fighting civilian population remains outside the hostilities. The civilian population is not an enemy and shall not be treated as an enemy, so long as it does not partake in battle. For sea war, on the contrary, at its basis lies the thought that the trade and economy of the enemy ought to be targeted. The enemy in such a war is not only the fighting opponent but also every member of an enemy state, and finally also the neutral party conducting trade with the enemy and who stands in an economic relation with the enemy. Land war has the tendency toward the decisive open battlefield. In sea war, it can also naturally come to a sea battle, but its typical means and methods are bombardment and blockade of enemy coasts and the seizure of enemy and neutral ships according to the right of capture.[110] It is grounded in the essence of these typical means of sea war that they may be directed at combatants as well as non-combatants. In particular, a blockade aiming at starvation strikes, without distinction, the whole population

---

110. Schmitt's term "Prisenrecht," the Latin equivalent of which is "ius praedae" and the subject of a treatise by Grotius, refers to the law of prize capture of enemy ships, the right of blockade, the right of the seizure of contraband, and the right of maritime control.

of the blockaded domain, the military and civilian population, men and women, the elderly and children.[111]

These are really not only two sides of an order in the law of peoples but rather two wholly different worlds. But, since the British appropriation of the sea, the English and those peoples under the spell of English ideas have accustomed themselves to this. The notion that a land power could exercise world power encompassing the whole globe was, according to their worldview, unheard of and unbearable. It was otherwise for a world dominion that was established on a maritime existence separated from the land and which encompassed the oceans of the world.[112] A small island on the northwest coast of Europe became the midpoint of a world empire by turning away from solid land and deciding for the sea.[113] In a purely maritime existence, it found the means of a world-dominion spread over the entire earth. After the separation of land and sea and the cleft of both elements had become the basic law of the planet, on

111. In the 1954 and 1981 editions, the following sentence from the 1942 edition has been omitted: "Die englische Auffassung sieht darin—weil der Hungertod ein unblutiger Tod ist—sogar einen Beweis höherer Menschlichkeit und verfeinerter Humanität, während ihr der 'Schlachtenkrieg' der kontinentalen Kriegführung als ein grausames Gemetzel vorkommt." This sentence might be rendered as follows: "In this the English disposition sees—because death by starvation is a bloodless death—even a proof of higher humanity and refined humaneness, while to it the 'battle-based war' of continental warfare appears as cruel butchery." Cf. Schmitt (1942), p. 62; Schmitt (1954), p. 51; Schmitt (1981), p. 88.

112. In the 1942 edition, this sentence was followed by two sentences removed from the 1954 and 1981 editions: "This appeared to them good and self-evident; this is for them the same thing as civilization and humanity; it is peace and the law of peoples itself. What is most astounding is that other peoples [*Völker*] took over such English concepts as classical truths." Cf. Schmitt (1942), p. 62; Schmitt (1954), p. 52; Schmitt (1981), p. 89.

113. In the 1942 and 1954 editions, this sentence began "A relatively [*verhältnismäßig*] small island on the northwest coast of Europe..." In the 1981 edition, the second word, "relatively" (*verhältnismäßig*), was removed. Cf. Schmitt (1942), p. 62; Schmitt (1954), p. 52; Schmitt (1981), p. 89.

this basis there arose a powerful framework of doctrines, propositional arguments, and scientific systems,[114] with which the wisdom and rationality of this condition was clarified, without recognizing the originary deed, the British appropriation of the sea and its time-bound character. Great scholars of national economy, jurists, and philosophers worked out such systems, and all this was very illuminating to most of our great-grandfathers. Finally, they no longer knew how to conceive any other economic science nor any other law of peoples. Here you can see that the great Leviathan has power even over the spirits and minds of humans. This is what is most astounding about its dominion.[115]

## 17

England is an island. However, only by first becoming the bearer and center of the elementary turn from the fixed land to the high sea, and only as the heiress of all the maritime energies released at that time, did it transform itself into the island, which is what one means when one ever and again intones that England is an island. And only in first becoming an island in a new, heretofore unknown sense did it complete the British maritime appropriation of the world oceans and complete the first phase of the planetary spatial revolution.

Obviously England is an island. But with the establishment of this geographic fact, not much has yet been said. There are many islands, the political destinies of which are entirely different. Sicily is an island, as are Ireland, Cuba, Madagascar,

114. In the 1942 and 1954 editions, this clause reads "and whole [*ganzen*] scientific systems," while in the 1981 edition, the term "whole" or "entire" (*ganzen*) has been removed. Schmitt (1942), p. 63; Schmitt (1954), p. 52; Schmitt (1981), p. 89.

115. In the 1942 and 1954 editions, this sentence reads: "This is that which is really [*wirklich*] most astounding about its dominion." In the 1981 edition, "really" (*wirklich*) has been removed. Cf. Schmitt (1942), p. 62; Schmitt (1954), p. 52; Schmitt (1981), p. 89.

and Japan. How many contradictory world-historical developments are already bound up with these few names, all of which name islands! In a certain sense, all continents, even the largest, are only islands, and the whole inhabited earth is, as the Greeks knew already, surrounded by the ocean. England itself since it separated itself from the continent millenia ago—perhaps 18,000 before our era[116]—has always been an island in the same way geographically under alternating historical destinies. It was an island when it was settled by the Celts and when it was conquered for Rome by Julius Caesar; it was an island with the Norman Conquest (1066) and at the time of the Virgin of Orleans (1431), when the English held the greater part of France under occupation.

The inhabitants of this island also had the feeling of a protected island situation. From the Middle Ages, beautiful poems and verses have been handed down to us in which England is celebrated as circumscribed by the sea like a fort surrounded by a protective moat. The most famous and most beautiful expression of this insular self-understanding is found in Shakespeare:

> This other Eden, this scepter'd isle, demi-paradise,
> This fortress built by Nature for herself
> This precious stone set in the silver sea
> Which serves it in the office of a wall
> Or as a moat defensive to a house.[117]

116. In the 1942 edition this clause between dashes reads: "etwa um 1800 vor unserer Zeitrechnung" ("around 1800 [years] before our era"). In the 1954 edition, "1800" is changed to "18000" and "around" (*etwa um*) is modified to "perhaps" (*vielleicht*), a change retained in the 1981 edition translated above. Cf. Schmitt (1942), p. 64; Schmitt (1954), p. 53; Schmitt (1981), p. 90.

117. Schmitt here cites, partially and rearranged, from the deathbed speech of John of Gaunt in Shakespeare's *Richard II*, act 2, scene 1, lines 31–68. The speech, in which the dying Gaunt laments the state of Richard II's England, begins with Gaunt's claim, "Methinks I am a prophet new inspired," and continues in lines 40–49 (from which Schmitt's citation is drawn):

It is understandable that the English often cite such verses and that in particular the turn of phrase "This precious stone set in the silver sea" could become a familiar expression.[118]

Such expressions of English island self-consciousness, however, belong to the old island. The island is still conceived as a piece of land sprung off from the continent, surrounded by the sea. This island-consciousness is still thoroughly landed, earthen, and territorial. It can even be that the island-feeling expresses itself as an especially territorial feeling for the earth. It would be an error to consider every island dweller and even today every English person as a born sea dog. Indeed, we saw already[119] what an alteration lies in the fact that a people of shepherds became a people of children of the sea in the

---

> This royal throne of kings, *this scepter'd isle*,
> This earth of majesty, this seat of Mars,
> *This other Eden, demi-paradise,*
> *This fortress built by Nature for herself*
> Against infection and the hand of war,
> This happy breed of men, this little world,
> *This precious stone set in the silver sea*
> *Which serves it in the office of a wall*
> *Or as a moat defensive to a house,*
> Against the envy of less happier lands,
> This blessed plot, this earth, this realm, this England

In this citation, Schmitt alters the speech of John of Gaunt in several respects. First, Schmitt interposes the end of line 40 ("this scepter'd isle") into the middle of line 42. Second, Schmitt omits lines 44–45, about nature blocking England from "infection and the hand of war" and the happiness of the English people, respectively. Third, Schmitt replaces the terminal comma with a period, breaking the citation at line 49, before line 50, which refers to England as the object of "the envy of less happier lands." In addition, Schmitt omits Shakespeare's reference to England as "this seat of Mars."

118. In the 1954 edition, this sentence, which follows the block quotation from Shakespeare's *Richard II*, is marked as a paragraph unto itself, which is not clear in the 1942 and 1981 editions, in which paragraph breaks are not preceded by an indentation.

119. In section 8 above. Cf. Schmitt (1942), pp. 31, 34; Schmitt (1954), pp. 26, 29; Schmitt (1981), pp. 46, 51.

sixteenth century. This was the fundamental transformation of the political-historical essence of the island itself. It consisted in the fact that the earth was now seen only from the perspective of the sea; the island, however, changed from a broken-off piece of the continent into a part of the sea, into a ship, or, even more significantly, into a fish.

A consistently and purely maritime perspective on the land is difficult for a territorial observer to comprehend. Our common language constructs its markers quite self-evidently from the land. We saw this already right at the beginning of our meditation.[120] We name the image that we make of our planet simply our image of the earth, and we forget that there can also be a sea-image of it. We speak, in relation to the sea, of sea lanes, although there are only traffic lines and no lanes as there are on land. We conceive of a ship on the high seas as a piece of land, which sails upon the sea as a "swimming piece of state domain," as one calls it in the treatment of this question in the law of peoples. A warship appears to us as a swimming fort, and an island like England appears to us encompassed by the sea like a fort surrounded by a moat. For maritime humans these are all entirely false transferences sprung from the imaginations of land rats. A ship is no swimming piece of land, as little as a fish is a swimming dog. Conversely, for a perspective oriented only by the sea, the fixed land is a mere coast, a beach with a "hinterland." Seen from the high sea and from the perspective of a maritime existence, even a whole land can be mere flotsam and an emission of the sea. An example, astounding for us but typical of this way of seeing from the sea, is a maxim of Edmund Burke, who said that Spain is nothing other than a whale-fish stranded on the shores of Europe.[121]

120. In section 1 above. Cf. Schmitt (1942), p. 6; Schmitt (1954), p. 5; Schmitt (1981), p. 10.

121. Schmitt sketches an earlier version of the argument of *Land and Sea* in his article "Das Meer gegen das Land" ("The Sea against the Land"), which

All essential relations with the rest of the world, in particular the relations to the states of the European continent as well, had to be transformed when England went over to a purely maritime existence. All measures and proportions of English politics now became incomparable and disunited from those of all the other[122] European lands. England became lady of the sea and erected upon its dominion over all the seas a British world empire spread over all parts of the earth. The English world thought in terms of base points and transport lines. That which was soil and home for other[123] peoples appeared to them as mere backcountry. The word "continental" acquired the connotation

---

was published in the journal *Das Reich*, on March 9, 1941. There, Schmitt writes: "What is Spain? asks Edmund Burke and gives an answer that the imagination of no continental European could find: Spain is a whale-fish [*Walfisch*] stranded on the shores of Europe." Carl Schmitt, "Das Meer gegen das Land," reprinted in *Staat, Großraum, Nomos*, pp. 395–400, at p. 397. The German editor of the 1995 edition comments on this passage: "This fine turn of phrase by Burke, oft deployed by Schmitt, could not be found to this day in Burke's work; Schmitt indeed uses a citation of Herman Melville from *Moby Dick*: 'Spain—a great whale stranded on the shores of Europe.'" Günter Maschke, "Anmerkungen des Herausgebers," to Schmitt, "Das Meer gegen das Land," in *Staat, Großraum, Nomos*, p. 399n[5]. Melville's "Sub-Sub Librarian" attributes the quotation to "*Edmund Burke (somewhere)*" in the opening section of quotations about whales and the Leviathan compiled as "Extracts (*Supplied by a Sub-Sub-Librarian*)" at the beginning of *Moby Dick*. Cf. Melville, *Moby Dick*, "Extracts (*Supplied by a Sub-Sub Librarian*)," p. xxxi: "'Spain—a great whale stranded on the shores of Europe.'—*Edmund Burke (somewhere)*." In the list of books present in Schmitt's postwar library maintained by Martin Tielke for the Carl-Schmitt-Gesellschaft, "Die Bibliothek Carl Schmitts (Monographien)," Stand: 14.05.2014, there are no works listed by Edmund Burke or works that mention Burke in the title. Cf. http://www.carl-schmitt.de/biblio-cs.php, accessed on April 15, 2015.

122. The orthography of "other" is different between the 1981 edition ("anderen") and the 1942 and 1954 editions ("andern"). Schmitt (1981), p. 93; Schmitt (1954), p. 55; Schmitt (1942), p. 66.

123. As in the previous note, here, the orthography of "other" is different between the 1981 edition ("anderen") and the 1942 and 1954 editions ("andern"). Schmitt (1981), p. 94; Schmitt (1954), p. 55; Schmitt (1942), p. 66.

of backward, and the populations belonging to it became "backward people."[124] The island itself, however, the metropolis of such a world empire erected upon purely maritime existence, thereby became uprooted and de-territorialized. Like a ship or a fish it can swim to another part of the earth as it is, indeed, only the transportable midpoint of a world empire spread over all continents lacking cohesion. Disraeli, the leading politician in the time of Queen Victoria, said in relation to India that the British[125] Empire is more an Asiatic[126] than a European power. It was also Disraeli who, in the year 1876, united the title of Queen of England with that of Empress of India. This act expresses the fact that the British world power drew its character as an empire from India. The same Disraeli had already made the suggestion in 1847 in his novel *Tancred* that the Queen of England should move to India. "The Queen should assemble a great fleet and with her whole court and the entire dominant class move out and remove the seat of her empire from London to Delhi. There she shall find a gigantic, finished empire, a first-class army, and great revenues."[127]

124. The phrase "backward people" is in English in Schmitt's German original in all three editions. Schmitt (1981), p. 94; Schmitt (1954), p. 55; Schmitt (1942), p. 66.
125. "British" in "British Empire" is capitalized in the 1954 and 1981 editions ("das Britische Reich") but not capitalized in the 1942 edition ("das britische Reich"). Schmitt (1981), p. 94; Schmitt (1954), p. 55; Schmitt (1942), p. 67.
126. "Asiatic" here translates Schmitt's term "asiatische." Schmitt (1981), p. 94; Schmitt (1954), p. 55; Schmitt (1942), p. 67.
127. Schmitt here appears to quote from Benjamin Disraeli's 1847 novel *Tancred: Or, The New Crusade*, 3 vols. (London: Henry Colburn, 1847), vol. 2, bk. 4, ch. 3, pp. 188–89. In the 1847 edition, the quotation is spoken by Disraeli's character Emir Fakredeen to Tancred: "with this steam, your ships have become a respectable Noah's ark. The game is up; Louis Philippe can take Windsor Castle whenever he pleases, as you took Acre, with the wind in his teeth. It is all over, then. Now, see a *coup d'état* that saves all. You must perform the Portuguese scheme on a grand scale; quit a petty and exhausted position for a vast and prolific Empire. Let the Queen of

82   CARL SCHMITT

Disraeli was an Abravanel (compare pp. 14–16 above)[128] of the nineteenth century.[129] Much of what[130] he said about the[131] race as the key to world history and about Judaism and

---

the English collect a great fleet, let her stow away all her treasure, bullion, gold plate and precious arms; be accompanied by all her court and chief people, and transfer the seat of her empire from London to Delhi. There she will find an immense empire ready made, a first-rate army, and a large revenue." Schmitt omits the part of the quotation dealing with "her treasure, bullion, gold plate and precious arms." Schmitt deploys this quotation (in a slightly different translation) in two articles from 1941, "Das Meer gegen das Land" and "Staatliche Souveränität und freies Meer," in the latter of which Schmitt appends a footnote giving his version of the English original (also omitting the part of the quotation referring to Queen Victoria's "treasure, bullion, gold plate and precious arms"). Cf. Schmitt, *Staat, Großraum, Nomos*, pp. 397, 399n[6], 421n22.

128. In the second paragraph in section 3 above.

129. In the 1942 edition, this sentence and the one that follows it reads quite differently than the text in the 1954 and 1981 editions. This passage explicitly cross-references Schmitt's discussions of Kabbalah and Abravanel in section 3, which was also altered and edited in both postwar editions. After explicitly comparing Disraeli to Abravanel ("Disraeli was an Abravanel of the nineteenth century"), Schmitt continues, "an initiate, an Elder of Zion" ("Disraeli war ein Abravanel (vgl. oben S. 10) des 19. Jahrhunderts, ein Eingeweihter, ein Weiser von Zion"). In the 1954 and 1981 editions, the last six words of this sentence were removed. Cf. Schmitt (1942), p. 67; Schmitt (1954), p. 56; Schmitt (1981), p. 95. In the 1942 edition, Schmitt calls Disraeli an "initiate" or "esotericist" (*ein Eingeweihter*) and labels the statesman as one of the "elders of Zion" (*ein Weiser von Zion*). Schmitt's term "Weiser von Zion" corresponds to the German title of the forged *Protocols of the Elders of Zion* (*Protokolle der Weisen von Zion*). Schmitt (1942), p. 67; Schmitt (1954), p. 56; Schmitt (1981), p. 95; Gross, *Carl Schmitt und die Juden*, p. 276; Meier, *Die Lehre Carl Schmitts*, p. 238. The 1942 version of the sentence is retained in the 1952 Spanish translation by Fernandez-Quintanilla; cf. Schmitt, *Tierra y Mar* (1952), p. 100.

130. In the 1981 edition of the work, the word translated as "what" (*was*) reads "was" (*war*). The 1954 text and the 1981 text of this sentence are identical with the exception that the 1954 text reads "what" (*was*) while the 1954 text reads "was" (*war*). The editors read "war" in the 1981 edition as a typographic or transcription error for "was," and translate this word according to the 1954 spelling. Schmitt (1954), p. 56; Schmitt (1981), p. 95.

131. The definite article is here retained to preserve an ambiguity in Schmitt's German, which may carry either a generic sense ("much of what

Christianity has been avidly propagated by non-Jews and non-Christians.[132] Thus, he knew what he said when he made such suggestions. He felt that the island was no longer a part of Europe. Its destiny was no longer necessarily bound up with that of Europe. It could break away and change its place as metropolis of a maritime world empire. The ship could lift anchor and lay anchor in another part of the earth. The great fish, the Leviathan, could set itself in motion and seek out other oceans.

## 18

After the Battle of Waterloo, when Napoleon was vanquished after twenty years of war, there began a period of England's full, uncontested rule of the sea. It lasted throughout the nineteenth century. In the middle of the century, after the Crimean War, and at the Paris Conference of 1856, which concluded the

---

he said about race") or an alternate, particular, sense ("much of what he said about the [Jewish] race").

132. This sentence, like the one that precedes it, reads quite differently in the 1942 edition, on the one hand, and in the 1954 and 1981 editions, on the other. In the 1942 edition, this sentence, following Schmitt's claim in the previous sentence that Disraeli was one of the "elders of Zion" (*ein Weiser von Zion*), might be translated as follows: "From him many sure on-target suggestions and formulations were emitted, which were avariciously absorbed by non-Jews" ("Von ihm sind viele zielsicheren Suggestionen und Formulierungen ausgegangen, die von Nichtjuden gierig aufgesogen wurden"). In the 1954 and 1981 editions, Schmitt changes "absorbed" (*aufgesogen*) to "propagated" (*propagiert*), adds "non-Christians" (*Nichtchristen*) to "non-Jews" (*Nichtjuden*), changes Disraeli's "target-sure suggestions and formulations" (*zielsicheren Suggestionen und Formulierungen*) to "what he said about race as key to world-history and [what he said] about Judaism and Christianity" (*wa[s] er über die Rasse als Schlüssel der Weltgeschichte und über Juden- und Christentum gesagt hat*), and changes "many" (*viele*) to "much" (*Manches*). Schmitt (1942), p. 67; Schmitt (1954), p. 56; Schmitt (1981), p. 95; Gross, *Carl Schmitt und die Juden*, p. 276; Meier, *Die Lehre Carl Schmitts*, p. 238 and 238nn90–91. The 1942 version of the sentence is retained in the 1952 Spanish translation by Fernandez-Quintanilla; cf. Schmitt, *Tierra y Mar* (1952), p. 100.

Crimean War, the high point was attained. The age of free trade was also the age of the free development of England's industrial and economic superiority. Free sea and free world market were united in a notion of freedom, the bearer and guardian of which could only be England. Around this time, the admiration and imitation of the English exemplar throughout the whole world reached its apex.

An inner transformation touched the elementary essence of the great Leviathan. Admittedly, at the time, this was not noticed. On the contrary. In consequence of the astounding world-economic boom, which now occurred, a positivist age, blinded by the rapidly growing wealth, believed that this wealth would always increase ever more and would flow into the millennial earthly paradise. The transformation, however, which touched the essence of the Leviathan, was a direct consequence of the industrial revolution. This had set in with the invention of machines in England in the eighteenth century. The first coal furnace (1735), the first cast-iron steel (1740), the steam engine (1768), the spinning jenny (1770), the mechanical loom (1786), all first in England, are several examples of England's great industrial advantage over all other peoples.[133] The steamship and the iron rail followed in the nineteenth century. Here, too, England remained in the lead. The great sea power simultaneously became the great machine power. Now its world dominion appeared to be final.

---

133. This passage is partially recapitulated in Schmitt's 1955 radio play *Dialogue on New Space (Gespräch über den Neuen Raum)*, in Schmitt, *Staat, Großraum, Nomos*, p. 560: "N[eumeyer]. We all know where the industrial revolution comes from. The industrial revolution comes from England in the eighteenth century. The dates are to be found in all school textbooks: the first coal furnace in 1735; the first cast-iron steel in 1740; the first steam-engine in 1768; the first modern factory in Nottingham in 1769; the first spinning jenny in 1770; the mechanical loom in 1786, and so on up to the first steam locomotive in 1825." Cf. Schmitt, *Dialogues on Power and Space*, pp. 67–68.

We saw above[134] how great the step is that the development of seafaring made in the few years between the sea battle of galleys at Lepanto (1571) and the annihilation of the Spanish Armada in the Channel (1588). An even greater step lay between the Crimean War, which England, France, and Sardinia waged against Russia in 1854–1856, and the American War of Secession, 1861 to[135] 1863,[136] in which the industrial Northern states vanquished the agrarian Southern states. The Crimean War was still conducted with battleships with sails, while the War of Secession was conducted with armored steamships. With this, the age of modern industrial and economic warfare begins. England, in any case, was still in the lead with this step and displayed its great advantage up until almost the end of the nineteenth century. But this step signified simultaneously a new stage in the elementary relation between land and sea.

Then, presently, the Leviathan transformed itself from a great fish into a machine. This was in fact an essential transformation of an extraordinary kind. The machine altered the relation of the humans to the sea. The daring type of men, which the grandeur of sea power had effected up to this time, lost its old sense. The bold achievements of seamanship on sailing ships, the high art of navigation, the harsh breed and selection of a particular type of men, all this paled in the security of modern technological sea transport. The sea always displayed

134. In section 4 above; cf. Schmitt (1981), p. 27.
135. In the 1942 edition, Schmitt marks his dating of the American Civil War with a dash "1861–1863"; in the 1954 and 1981 editions, Schmitt changes the dash to "to" or "until" (bis) ("1861 bis 1863"). Schmitt (1942), p. 69; Schmitt (1954), p. 57; Schmitt (1981), p. 97.
136. In all three editions published in his lifetime, Schmitt refers to the American Civil War as "the American War of Secession" ("dem amerikanischen Sezessionskrieg") and dates the war between 1861 and 1863, instead of 1861 to 1865. Schmitt's dating may seem to fix the conclusion of the war (in Schmitt's view) with the decisive Battle of Gettysburg, fought in July 1863. Schmitt (1942), p. 69; Schmitt (1954), p. 57; Schmitt (1981), p. 97.

its human-forming force. But the further efficaciousness of this powerful impulse, which had transformed a people of shepherds into pirates, abated and finally ceased. Between the element of the sea and human existence, a mechanized apparatus was introduced. A dominion over the sea erected upon mechanized industry is manifestly something other than a sea power, which is attained every day in the hardest unmediated battle with the element. A sailing ship, which is operated only by human muscular force, and a ship propelled by steam wheels already represent two different relationships to the element of the sea. The industrial revolution transformed the children of the sea[137] born from the element of the sea into machine builders and machine attendants.

Everyone felt the transformation. Some complained about the end of the old, heroic age and fled into the romanticism of the stories of sea robbers. Others were jubilant about the progress of technology and plunged into the utopias of constructed human paradises. Here we are showing in all materiality that the purely maritime existence, the secret of British world power, was struck at its essential core. But the humans of the nineteenth century paid no notice. Then, whether fish or machine, the Leviathan, in any case, became ever stronger and more powerful and its empire appeared to have no end.

## 19

The American Admiral Mahan made a curious attempt to perpetuate the originary situation of the British appropriation of the seas at the end of the nineteenth and at the beginning of

---

137. Cf. Hosea 11:10 in the Latin Vulgate: "post Dominum ambulabunt quasi leo rugiet quia ipse rugiet et formidabunt filii maris." Hosea 11:10 is rendered in the Douay-Rheims translation as follows: "They shall walk after the Lord, he shall roar as a lion: because he shall roar, and the children of the sea shall fear."

the twentieth centuries. Mahan is an important historiographer of the "Influence of Sea Power in History." Thus he titled his major work, which also appeared[138] in German and which found the recognition of the German navy, especially its creator, the Grand Admiral von Tirpitz.

In an article from July 1904, Mahan speaks of the possibilities of a reunification of England with the United States of America. The deepest reason of such a reunification he sees not in the common race or language or culture. He in no way underestimates these perspectives often put forth by other writers. But they are to him only welcome side effects. For him what is decisive is that the Anglo-Saxon dominion over the seas of the world must be upheld, and that can only happen on an "insular" basis through a union of both Anglo-American powers. England itself, however, has become too small as a result of modern development and is thus no longer the island in the same sense. The United States of America, by contrast, is the true island of the times. This has, Mahan says, not come to consciousness as a result of its extent. However, it corresponds to contemporary measures and proportions. The insular character of the United States shall be the cause that perpetuates and furthers the dominion over the seas on a broader basis. America is the great island out of which the British appropriation of the seas shall be eternalized and advanced in grander style as Anglo-American sea dominion over the world.

While a politician like Disraeli[139] wanted to remove the British world empire to Asia, the American admiral had in

138. In the 1981 edition, the tense of "appeared" is preterite (praeteritum) (*erschien*) where it had been perfect ("has appeared") in the 1954 and 1942 editions (*erschienen ist*). Schmitt (1942), p. 71; Schmitt (1954), p. 59; Schmitt (1981), p. 100.

139. In the 1942 edition, the beginning of this sentence reads, "While the Jewish politician Disraeli wanted to remove the British world empire to Asia." Schmitt (1942), p. 72. In the 1954 and 1981 editions, Schmitt's phrase

mind a move to America. This lies in the orientation of a way of thinking that was natural to an Anglo-Saxon marine man of the nineteenth century. The admiral felt the transformation of the age; he saw the violent alterations of masses and measures, which inevitably accompanied industrial development. However, he did not see that the industrial transformation hit precisely the essential point, the elementary relation of the humans to the sea. Thus it transpires that he continues to think in the old line. His greater island aims to conserve a received, aging tradition in a fully new situation. The old, too

---

"*the Jewish* politician Disraeli" ("der jüdische Politiker Disraeli") has been changed to "*a* politician *like* Disraeli" ("ein Politiker wie Disraeli"). In 1936, Schmitt argued that all Jewish sources in legal and academic writings should be explicitly marked as such (*Die deutsche Rechtswissenschaft im Kampf gegen den jüdischen Geist*, p. 16), a principle of Schmitt's that may seem to be operative in the 1942 edition of this passage. While the 1952 Spanish translation of *Land and Sea* had retained Schmitt's reference to Disraeli as an "elder of Zion," here the 1952 Spanish translation by Fernandez-Quintanilla removes the modifier that Disraeli is a "*Jewish* politician" without adopting the 1954 and 1981 German variants of the passage. In this passage in the 1952 Spanish translation, the text reads: "While the politician Disraeli wanted to translate the English Empire to Asia" ("Mientras el político Disraeli quería trasladar al Asia el Imperio inglés"). Schmitt, *Tierra y Mar* (1952), p. 107. Cf. Carl Schmitt, *Das Judentum in der Rechtswissenschaft, Die deutsche Rechtswissenschaft im Kampf gegen den jüdischen Geist* (Berlin: Deutscher Rechtsverlag, 1936), pp. 14–17, at p. 16: "We owe to racial theory [*Rassenlehre*] the distinction between the Jews and other peoples. The French, the English, and the Italians have exercised great influence upon us. Within this there are good and evil influences. But always there is in such an influence of Aryan peoples something fully other than the influence of the Jewish spirit. We are speaking here, where the concern is the Jews, not, in general, of 'Non-Aryans.' Thereby the Jew is placed into a society, in which he finds unexpected allies and quite possibly may advance arm in arm with grand samurais and knightly Magyars. Then he has the possibility to denounce the battle against the Jewish people as a battle against other non-Jewish peoples and set his German-inimical propaganda [*deutschfeindliche Propaganda*] under a new aspect. Finally, we are not speaking of the Jewish people as one of the 'National minorities.'...We are thus speaking of the Jews and calling them by their name."

small[140] island and the whole complex of a sea power and a world power erected upon it should be connected to the new island and saved by it, as if by a mountainous rescue ship.

However significant Mahan's personality is and however impressive his construction of the greater island may be, it does not get to the elementary core of a new spatial order. It is not borne out of the spirit of the old seafarers. It comes from a conservative need for geopolitical security and has nothing more of the energies of the elementary rupture that, in the sixteenth and seventeenth centuries, established the world-historical union between daring seafaring and the Calvinist belief in predestination.

## 20

Industrial development and new technology did not remain fixed in their nineteenth-century position. They did not stick with the steamship and the iron rail. Faster[141] than even the most machine-credulous prophets had imagined, the world transformed and entered the age of electric technology and electrodynamics. Electricity, flight, and radio effected such a transformation of all conceptions of space that, manifestly, a new stage of the first planetary spatial revolution, if not even a second new spatial revolution, had set in.

Within a few years, in the period from 1890 to 1914, a state of the European continent, Germany, caught up with the English advantage and in important domains in mechanical, nautical,

---

140. In the 1942 edition, this sentence begins, "The old, decaying island" ("Die alte, vergehende Insel"), which was changed to "The old, too small island" ("Die alte, zu kleine Insel") in the 1954 and 1981 editions. Schmitt (1942), p. 72; Schmitt (1954), p. 60; Schmitt (1981), pp. 101–2.

141. "Faster" (*Schneller*) is followed by a comma in the 1981 edition, but not in the 1954 or 1942 editions. Schmitt (1942), p. 73; Schmitt (1954), p. 60; Schmitt (1981), p. 103.

locomotive engineering even surpassed it, after Krupp had proven to be a match for the English already in the year 1868 in the domain of ordnance manufacture. The 1914 World War already stood under the new sign. Admittedly, the peoples and their governments tumbled into a spatial revolutionary age without the consciousness of being in one, as if they were dealing with one of their familiar wars from the nineteenth century. In highly industrialized Germany, English constitutional ideals still reigned and English concepts were held to be classical concepts, while a gigantic agrarian country, Czarist Russia, began the First World War in 1914 without possession of a single modern motor factory of its own anywhere on its expansive soil. In reality, the step from the steamship to the modern battleship was no smaller than that from the oar-powered galley to the sailing ship. The relation of the humans to the element of the sea was most deeply altered once again.

When the airplane came in, a new, third dimension was conquered, in addition to land and sea. Now the human raised itself above the surfaces of the land as above the surfaces of the sea and received a fully novel means of transport and an equally new weapon in its hands. The weights and measures transformed themselves further, and the possibilities for human dominion over nature ascended into innumerable domains. It is understandable that precisely the air force [*Luftwaffe*] is designated as a "space force" [*Raumwaffe*]. And, indeed, the spatial revolutionary effect that proceeds from it is particularly strong, immediate, and plain to see.

If, in addition, one imagines not only that airplanes fly through the airspace over land and sea but also that radio waves from transmissions from all lands circle the globe uninterruptedly through the atmospheric space, then it would be easy to believe now not only that a new, third dimension has been achieved but also that even a third element has been added, the *air*,[142] as a new elementary domain of human existence. To both the mythic beasts, Leviathan and Behemoth, a third would be added, a great bird. But we must not be overhasty with such consequential propositions. Indeed, if one thinks of the mechanized technical means and energies with which human power is exercised in airspace, and if one recognizes the explosive motors by means of which air machines are moved, then it appears that it is the *fire*[143] that is the additional, genuinely new element of human activity.

The question of both the new elements, additions to land and sea, shall not be decided here. Here, serious suggestions and fantastic speculations are still very much intermingled and have an immeasurable space of play. According to an ancient doctrine,[144] the whole history of humanity is, indeed, only a journey through the four elements. Let us, however, stick soberly to our theme, and thus there are for us two possible material and

142. "Air" (*Luft*) is italicized in all three German editions. Cf. Schmitt (1942), pp. 74–75; Schmitt (1954), p. 62; Schmitt (1981), p. 105.

143. "Fire" (*Feuer*) is italicized in all three German editions. Cf. Schmitt (1942), p. 75; Schmitt (1954), p. 62; Schmitt (1981), p. 105.

144. Schmitt may here refer to Diels-Kranz fragments 14.1 (Herodotus II.123) and 31 B 117 (Diogenes Laertius VIII.77). Schmitt had a postwar edition of *Die Fragmente der Vorsokratiker* in his postwar library: "Diels, Hermann: Die Fragmente der Vorsokratiker. Mit Einführungen u. Bibliographien von Gert Plamböck. Nach d. von Walther Kranz hrsg., 8. Aufl. (Rowohlts Klassiker der Literatur und der Wissenschaft, 10), Hamburg 1957." Schmitt also held two volumes of Herodotus in his postwar library: "Herodotus: Historien. Deutsch v. August Horneffer (Antike Kultur, 14), Leipzig 1910 Semmel Nr. 323 Herodotus: Herodoti Historiarum libri IX. Cur. Henr. Rudolph Dietsch. Fasc. 2. Lib. III. IV. Ed. ster. (= Historiae. Curavit curatamque em. H. Kallenberg) (Bibliotheca scriptorum Graecorum et Romanorum Teubneriana), Lipsiae 1911." Tielke, "Die Bibliothek Carl Schmitts (Monographien)," pp. 91, 186; cf. Mansfeld and Primavesi, eds., *Die Vorsokratiker, Griechisch und Deutsch*, pp. 172–73, 176–77. In a letter to Schmitt dated June 8, 1938, Ernst Jünger notes that a visit to Rhodes has awakened in him a hunger to read Herodotus. Jünger–Schmitt, *Briefe 1930–1983*, p. 75.

sure conclusions. The first relates to the transformation of the concept of space, which begins with the new stage of the spatial revolution. This transformation is no less deep than that of the sixteenth and seventeenth centuries, with which we have become acquainted. At that time, humans found the world to be in an empty space. Today, by space we no longer understand a mere dimension of depth, empty of every conceivable content. For us, space has become a force field of human energy, activity, and achievement. Today, a thought first becomes possible for us that would have been impossible in any other epoch and which a contemporary German philosopher has articulated: The world is not in space, rather space is in the world.[145]

145. Here, in claiming that a "contemporary German philosopher" argues that "Die Welt ist nicht im Raum, sondern der Raum ist in der Welt," Schmitt appears to refer to sections 22, 24, and 70 of Martin Heidegger's 1927 treatise *Sein und Zeit*, in which Heidegger claims (section 24): "*Der Raum ist weder im Subjekt, noch ist die Welt im Raum. Der Raum ist vielmehr 'in' der Welt, sofern das für das Dasein konstitutive In-der-Welt-sein Raum erschlossen hat.*" Martin Heidegger, *Sein und Zeit, Erste Hälfte* (Sonderdruck aus "Jahrbuch für Philosophie und phänomenologische Forschung," Band VIII, herausgegeben von E. Husserl) (Halle an der Saale: Max Niemeyer Verlag, 1927), p. 111. Cf. Martin Heidegger, *Being and Time*, trans. Joan Stambaugh, rev. ed. (Albany: SUNY Press, 2010), p. 109. In other passages of *Sein und Zeit*, Heidegger claims (section 70) that "*Die Welt ist nicht im Raum* vorhanden; dieser jedoch läßt sich nur innerhalb einer Raum entdecken." Heidegger, *Sein und Zeit*, sect. 70, "Die Zeitlichkeit der Daseinsmäßigen Räumlichkeit," p. 369. Schmitt also might seem to draw on Heidegger's claim (section 22) that "*Der Raum, der im umsichtigen In-der-Welt-sein als Räumlichkeit des Zeugganzen entdeckt ist, gehört je als dessen Platz zum Seienden selbst.*" Heidegger, *Sein und Zeit*, sect. 22, "Die Räumlichkeit des innerweltlichen Zuhandenen," p. 104. Cf. Carl Schmitt, *Terra e Mare, Una riflessione sulla storia del mondo*, trans. Giovanni Gurisatti, 5th ed. (Milan: Adelphi Edizioni, 2011 [2002]), p. 109n1. On this passage, Eduardo Mendieta comments: "Schmitt quotes Heidegger without directly naming him.... Schmitt is here paraphrasing Heidegger's statement in *Being and Time*: '*Space is neither in the subject nor is the world in space. Rather, space is 'in' the world since the being-in-the-world constitutive for Da-sein has disclosed space.*'" Cf. Eduardo Mendieta,

Our second conclusion touches the elementary relation between land and sea. The sea is today no longer an element as it was in the time of the whale hunters and corsairs. Today's transportation and communications technology has made the sea into a space in the contemporary sense of the word. Today, in times of peace, every shipowner can know daily and hourly at which point in the ocean his ship on the high sea is to be found. With this, in contrast to the age of sail ships, the world of the sea is elementarily altered for humans. However, if this is so, then the division of sea and land, upon which the link between sea domination and world domination allowed itself to be erected, falls away. The basis of British sea appropriation falls away, and, with it, what had up till now been the *nomos* of the earth.

In its place the new *nomos* of our planet grows, unceasingly and irresistibly. It is summoned by the new relations of humans to the old and to the new elements, and the altered measurements and relations of human existence compel it.[146] Many shall see in it only death and destruction. Some believe themselves to be experiencing the end of the world. In reality we are only experiencing the end of the relation between land and sea, which had held up to this point. Still, human angst [*Angst*] in the face of the new is often as great as the angst in the face of the void, even when the new is the overcoming of the void. Thus, the many see only senseless disorder, where, in reality, a new sense struggles for its order. Admittedly, the old *nomos* falls away and with it a whole system of received measures, norms, and relations. But that which is coming is not therefore only

---

"*Land and Sea*," in *Spatiality, Sovereignty and Carl Schmitt: Geographies of the nomos*, ed. Stephen Legg (London: Routledge, 2011), pp. 260–67, at p. 263.

146. In between this sentence and the sentence that follows, a six-word sentence, present in the 1942 edition but absent in both post–World War II editions, reads: "Only in battle can it emerge" ("Nur im Kampf kann er entstehen"). Schmitt (1942), p. 76; Schmitt (1954), p. 63; Schmitt (1981), p. 107.

measurelessness or a nothingness hostile to *nomos*. Even in the embittered struggle[147] of old and new forces, just measures emerge and sensible proportions are constructed.

> Here, too, there are Gods and Gods hold sway,
> Great is their mass.[148]

147. In the 1942 edition, this sentence begins "Even in the cruel war of old and new forces" ("Auch in dem grausamen Krieg alter und neuer Kräfte"), which has been altered in the 1954 and 1981 editions to "Even in the embittered struggle of old and new forces" ("Auch in dem erbitterten Ringen alter und neuer Kräfte"). In both post–World War II editions, "cruel war" has been replaced with "embittered struggle." Schmitt (1942), p. 76; Schmitt (1954), p. 63; Schmitt (1981), p. 107.

148. A partial excerpt from this paragraph in the 1942 edition was translated in Jan-Werner Müller's 2003 monograph *A Dangerous Mind: Carl Schmitt in Post-War European Thought* (New Haven, CT: Yale Univ. Press, 2003), p. 46: "only in struggle can the new *nomos* arise. Many see in it only death and destruction. Some believe that they are experiencing the end of the world. In reality we are experiencing only the end of the former relationship between land and sea.... Also in the cruel war of old and new powers, just measures arise and meaningful proportions form. Here, too, gods are and rule / Great is their measure." Cf. Müller, *A Dangerous Mind*, p. 256n88. Müller notes that terminal couplet is drawn from Hölderlin, without specifying the poem: "The last lines, drawn from the German poet Hölderlin, foreshadowed a final shift from elemental mythology to eschatology." Müller, *A Dangerous Mind*, p. 46. Schmitt here appears to quote from part of the last two lines of the first stanza of the second version of Friedrich Hölderlin's poem "The Wanderer" (*Der Wanderer, Zweite Fassung*).

# Afterword[1]

"As the earth, fixed *ground* and *soil*, is the condition for the principle of family life, so for industry the outward enlivening element is the sea."

—Hegel, *Elements of the Philosophy of Right*, § 247[2]

I leave it to the attentive reader to find in my exertions the beginning of an attempt to bring to fulfilment this § 247 in a way similar to that in which §§ 243–246 was brought to fulfilment in Marxism.[3]

Carl Schmitt<br>April 10, 1981

The first edition of this book appeared in Leipzig in 1942, the second in Stuttgart in 1954.

---

1. This "Afterword" (*Nachbemerkung*) was added to the 1981 edition of *Land und Meer* published by "Hohenheim" Verlag in the series Edition Maschke in Cologne, and is not present in the two editions published by Reclam in 1942 and 1954, respectively. In the 1942 edition, in place of an "Afterword," there is an "Overview" (*Überblick*), which has been translated as an appendix to the present edition, but which is absent in both the 1954 and 1981 editions.

2. Cf. G. W. F. Hegel, *Grundlinien der Philosophie des Rechts oder Naturrecht und Staatswissenschaft im Grundrisse* (Frankfurt am Main: Suhrkamp, 1986 [1970]), pp. 391 ff. In Hegel's original the quotation runs: "As the earth, fixed *ground* and *soil*, is the condition for the principle of family life, so for industry the outward enlivening *natural* [*natürliche*] element is the sea" (italics added). Schmitt's quotation omits the word "natural" [*natürliche*]. In the following paragraph, § 248 of the *Elements of the Philosophy of Right*, Hegel treats maritime and overseas colonization.

3. An earlier version of the claims in this afterword was published in Schmitt's 1955 contribution to Ernst Jünger's Festschrift, "Die geschichtliche Struktur des heutigen Welt-Gegensatzes von Ost und West: Bemerkungen

zu Ernst Jüngers Schrift: 'Der Gordische Knoten,'" in Armin Mohler, ed., *Freundschaftliche Begegnungen: Festschrift für Ernst Jünger zum 60. Geburtstag* (Frankfurt am Main: Vittorio Klostermann, 1955), pp. 133–67, at pp. 163–67, reprinted in *Staat, Großraum, Nomos*, pp. 523–51, at pp. 543–44. Schmitt also articulated the claims in this afterword in a note to his 1963 tract *Theory of the Partisan*. Cf. Carl Schmitt, *Theory of the Partisan*, trans. G. L. Ulmen (New York: Telos Press, 2007 [1975/1963]), p. 21n32. Schmitt also quotes this passage from Hegel in his 1950 treatise, *The Nomos of the Earth*. Cf. Schmitt, *Der Nomos der Erde im Völkerrecht des Jus Publicum Europaeum*, 5th ed. (Berlin: Duncker & Humblot, 2011 [1950]), p. 20; Schmitt, *The Nomos of the Earth*, p. 49.

# Appendix: Overview [*Übersicht*][1]

1. First glance at land and sea
2. What is an element?
3. The land against the sea
4. From the coast into the ocean
5. In praise of the whale and of the whale-hunter
6. From the oar to the sail
7. Pirates and sea dogs
8. History of the Lady Killigrew
9. England as the heir of European achievements at sea
10. What is a spatial revolution?
11. Three world-historical examples
12. The first planetary spatial revolution
13. European land-appropriation of the New World
14. The battle between the land-appropriators
15. Land and sea in the War of Religion
16. British sea-appropriation and the separation of land and sea
17. Transformation of the essence of the island
18. From the fish to the machine
19. Mahan's greater island
20. The new stage of the planetary spatial revolution

---

1. The 1942 edition of *Land und Meer* (Leipzig: Reclam, 1942) concludes with an "Overview" (*Übersicht*) that functions as a concluding or summary table of contents (p. [77]), absent from the 1954 and 1981 (and subsequent) editions. In Giovanni Gurisatti's 2002 Italian translation, the "Overview" (*Übersicht*) is translated as an opening table of contents ("Indice"), and each of the headings is reproduced as a chapter title before each section. Cf. Carl Schmitt, *Terra e Mare: Una riflessione sulla storia del mondo*, trans. Giovanni Gurisatti, 5th ed. (Milan: Adelphi Edizioni, 2011 [2002]), pp. 7, 11, 15.

# Works Consulted

## German Editions of *Land und Meer*

Schmitt, Carl. *Land und Meer: Eine weltgeschichtliche Betrachtung.* Leipzig: Verlag von Philipp Reclam jun., 1942.

Schmitt, Carl. *Land und Meer: Eine weltgeschichtliche Betrachtung.* New rev. ed. Stuttgart: Reclam Verlag, 1954.

Schmitt, Carl. *Land und Meer: Eine weltgeschichtliche Betrachtung.* 3rd ed. Cologne: Hohenheim Verlag/Edition Maschke, 1981.

Schmitt, Carl. *Land und Meer: Eine weltgeschichtliche Betrachtung.* 7th ed. Stuttgart: Klett-Cotta, 2011.

## Spanish Edition of *Land und Meer*

Schmitt, Carl. *Tierra y Mar: Consideraciones sobre la historia universal.* Translated by Rafael Fernandez-Quintanilla. Madrid: Instituto de Estudios Políticos (Series: Colección Civitas), 1952.

## French Edition of *Land und Meer*

Schmitt, Carl. *Terre et Mer: Un point de vue sur l'histoire mondiale.* Introduction and afterword by Julien Freund. Translated by Jean-Louis Pesteil. Paris: Éditions du Labyrinthe, 1985.

## Italian Edition of *Land und Meer*

Schmitt, Carl. *Terra e Mare: Una riflessione sulla storia del mondo.* 5th ed. Translated by Giovanni Gurisatti. Milan: Adelphi Edizioni, 2011 [2002].

## Works Referenced by Carl Schmitt in *Land and Sea*

Burckhardt, Jakob. *Weltgeschichtliche Betrachtungen*. Edited by Rudolf Marx. Leipzig: Kröners, n.d.

Chroust, Anton, ed. *Briefe und Akten zur Geschichte des Dreissigjährigen Krieges in den Zeiten des Vorwaltenden Einflusses der Wittelsbacher*. 12 vols. Munich: M. Riegersche Universitäts-Buchhandlung, 1906.

Corbett, Julian S. *Some Principles of Maritime Strategy*. New ed. London: Longmans, Green, and Co., 1918.

Disraeli, Benjamin. *Tancred: Or, The New Crusade*. 3 vols. London: Henry Colburn, 1847.

Gosse, Philip. *The Pirates' Who's Who, Giving the Particulars of the Lives & Deaths of Pirates and Buccaneers*. Boston: Lauriat, 1924.

Gosse, Philip. *The History of Piracy*. London: Longmans, Green, & Co., 1932.

Grillparzer, Franz. *Ein Bruderzwist in Habsburg: Trauerspiel in 5 Aufz*. Leipzig: Insel Verlag, 1941.

Hagedorn, Bernhard. *Die Entwicklung der wichtigsten Schiffstypen bis ins 19. Jh*. Berlin: Curtius, 1914.

Hegel, G. W. F. *Grundlinien der Philosophie des Rechts oder Naturrecht und Staatswissenschaft im Grundrisse*. Frankfurt am Main: Suhrkamp, 1986 [1970].

Hegel, G. W. F. *Die Phänomenologie des Geistes*. Vol. 2 of *Sämtliche Werke: kritische Gesamtausgabe der Werke Hegels in zwölf Bänden*. Edited and introduced by Otto Weiß. Leipzig: 1909.

Heidegger, Martin. *Being and Time*. Translated by Joan Stambaugh. Rev. ed. Albany: SUNY Press, 2010.

Heidegger, Martin. *Sein und Zeit: Erste Hälfte*. Reprinted from *Jahrbuch für Philosophie und phänomenologische Forschung*, vol. 8, edited by E. Husserl. Halle an der Saale: Max Niemeyer Verlag, 1927.

Heine, Heinrich. "Disputation." From *Romanzero, Drittes Buch: Hebräische Melodien* (1851). In *Sämtliche Gedichte: Kommentierte Ausgabe*, edited by Bernd Kortländer, pp. 646–62. Stuttgart: Philipp Reclam jun., 2009 [1990].

Kapp, Ernst. *Philosophische oder Vergleichende Allgemeine Erdkunde als Wissenschaftliche Darstellung der Erdverhältnisse und des Menschenlebens nach ihrem inneren Zusammenhang*. 2 vols. Braunschweig: Verlag von Georg Westermann, 1845.

Melville, Herman. *Moby Dick*. New York: Penguin Books, 2001.

Melville, Herman. *Moby Dick oder der weiße Wal. Roman*. Translated and edited by Wilhelm Strüver. Berlin: [1927].

Michelet, Jules. *La mer*. 2nd. ed. Paris: Librairie de L. Hachette, 1861.

Raleigh Walter. *The Works of Sir Walter Ralegh, Kt.: Political, Commercial, and Philosophical; Together with his Letters and Poems. The whole never before collected together, and some never yet printed. To which is prefix'd, a new account of his life by Tho. Birch* 2 vols. London: R. Dodsley, 1751.

Rörig, Fritz. *Mittelalterliche Weltwirtschaft: Blüte und Ende einer Weltwirtschaftsperiode*. Jena: G. Fischer, 1933.

Schramm, Percy Ernst. *Geschichte des englischen Königtums im Lichte der Krönung*. Weimar: Verlag Hermann Böhlhaus Nachfolger, 1937.

Seneca. *L. Annaei Senecae Tragoediae*. Rec. Rudolfus Peiper et Gustavus Richter. Bibliotheca scriptorum Graecorum et Romanorum Teubneriana. Lipsiae, 1937.

Shakespeare, William. *Sämtliche Werke in einem Bande*. Vienna: [ca. 1840].

### Editions of Other Works by Schmitt in German

Schmitt, Carl. *Gesetz und Urteil: Eine Untersuchung zum Problem der Rechtspraxis.* 2nd ed. Munich: Verlag C. H. Beck, 1969 [1912].

[Schmitt, Carl.] Johannes Negelinus. *Schattenrisse* [1913]. In Ingeborg Villinger, *Carl Schmitts Kulturkritik der Moderne: Text, Kommentar und Analyse der "Schattenrisse" des Johannes Negelinus*, pp. 11–67. Berlin: Akademie Verlag, 1995.

Schmitt, Carl. *Der Wert des Staates und die Bedeutung des Einzelnen.* 2nd ed. Berlin: Duncker & Humblot, 2004 [1914].

Schmitt, Carl. *Theodor Däublers "Nordlicht" Drei Studien über die Elemente, den Geist und die Aktualität des Werkes.* 3rd ed. Berlin: Duncker & Humblot, 2009 [1916].

Schmitt, Carl. *Politische Theologie.* 9th ed. Berlin: Duncker & Humblot, 2009 [1922/1934].

Schmitt, Carl. *Römischer Katholizismus und politische Form.* 5th ed. Stuttgart: Klett-Cotta, 2008 [1923/1925].

Schmitt, Carl. *Verfassungslehre.* 10th ed. Berlin: Duncker & Humblot, 2010 [1928].

Schmitt, Carl. *Der Begriff des Politischen: Text von 1932 mit einem Vorwort und drei Corollarien.* 8th ed. Berlin: Duncker & Humblot, 2009 [1932].

Schmitt, Carl. *Über die drei Arten des rechtswissenschaftlichen Denkens.* 3rd ed. Berlin: Duncker & Humblot, 2006 [1934].

Schmitt, Carl. "Eröffnung der wissenschaftlichen Vorträge durch den Reichsgruppenwalter Staatsrat Prof. Dr. Carl Schmitt." In *Das Judentum in der Rechtswissenschaft, Ansprachen, Vorträge und Ergebnisse der Tagung der Reichsgruppe Hochschullehrer des NSRB. am 3. und 4. Oktober 1936, 1. Die deutsche Rechtswissenschaft im Kampf gegen den Jüdischen Geist*, pp. 14–17. Berlin: Deutscher Rechtsverlag, 1936.

Schmitt, Carl. *Der Leviathan in der Staatslehre des Thomas Hobbes: Sinn und Fehlschlag eines politischen Symbols.* 4th ed. Stuttgart: Klett-Cotta, 2012 [1938].

Schmitt, Carl. *Die Wendung zum Diskriminierenden Kriegsbegriff.* 4th ed. Berlin: Duncker & Humblot, 2007 [1938].

Schmitt, Carl. *Positionen und Begriffe im Kampf mit Weimar—Genf—Versailles 1923–1939.* 4th rev. ed. Berlin: Duncker & Humblot, 2014 [1940].

Schmitt, Carl. *Völkerrechtliche Großraumordnung mit Interventionsverbot für raumfremde Mächte: Ein Beitrag zum Reichsbegriff im Völkerrecht.* 3rd unrevised ed. of 1941 ed. Berlin: Duncker & Humblot, 2009 [1941].

Schmitt, Carl. *Land und Meer: Eine weltgeschichtliche Betrachtung.* Leipzig: Reclam, 1942.

Schmitt, Carl. *Ex Captivitate Salus: Erfahrungen der Zeit 1945/47.* 3rd ed. Berlin: Duncker & Humblot, 2010 [1950].

Schmitt, Carl. *Donoso Cortés in gesamteuropäischer Interpretation: Vier Aufsätze.* 2nd ed. Berlin: Duncker & Humblot, 2009 [1950].

Schmitt, Carl. *Der Nomos der Erde im Völkerrecht des Jus Publicum Europaeum.* 5th ed. Berlin: Duncker & Humblot, 2011 [1950].

Schmitt, Carl. *Land und Meer: Eine weltgeschichtliche Betrachtung.* New rev. ed. Stuttgart: Reclam, 1954.

Schmitt, Carl. *Gespräch über die Macht und den Zugang zum Machthaber.* Stuttgart: Klett-Cotta, 2008 [1954].

Schmitt, Carl. *Hamlet oder Hecuba: Der Einbruck der Zeit in das Spiel.* 5th ed. Stuttgart: Klett-Cotta, 2008 [1956].

Schmitt, Carl. "Prolog zu 'Diálogos' (Madrid 1962)." Translated by Günter Maschke. In Piet Tommissen, ed., *Schmittiana: Beiträge zu Leben und Werk Carl Schmitts,* vol. 5, pp. 21–22. Berlin: Duncker & Humblot, 1996.

Schmitt, Carl. *Die Tyrannei der Werte*. 3rd rev. ed. Berlin: Duncker & Humblot, 2011 [1967].

Schmitt, Carl. *Politische Theologie II: Die Legende der Erledigung jeder Politischen Theologie*. 5th ed. Berlin: Duncker & Humblot, 2008 [1970].

Schmitt, Carl. *Das internationalrechtliche Verbrechen des Angriffskrieges und der Grundsatz "Nullum crimen, nulla poena sine lege"*. Edited by Helmut Quaritsch. Berlin: Duncker & Humblot, 1994.

Schmitt, Carl. *Staat, Großraum, Nomos: Arbeiten aus den Jahren 1916–1969*. Edited by Günter Maschke. Berlin: Duncker & Humblot, 1995.

Schmitt, Carl. *Antworten in Nürnberg*. Edited by Helmut Quaritsch. Berlin: Duncker & Humblot, 2000.

Schmitt, Carl, and Álvaro d'Ors. *Briefwechsel*. Edited by Montserrat Herrero. Berlin: Duncker & Humblot, 2004.

Schmitt, Carl. *Frieden oder Pazifismus? Arbeiten zum Völkerrecht und zur internationalen Politik 1924–1978*. Edited by Günter Maschke. Berlin: Duncker & Humblot, 2005.

Schmitt, Carl, and Gretha Jünger. *Briefwechsel (1934–1953)*. Edited by Ingeborg Villinger and Alexander Jaser. Berlin: Akademie Verlag, 2007.

Forsthoff, Ernst, and Carl Schmitt. *Briefwechsel (1926–1974)*. Edited by Dorothee Mußgnug, Reinhard Mußgnug, and Angela Reinthal. Berlin: Akademie Verlag, 2007.

Schmitt, Carl, and Ernst Jünger. *Briefe 1930–1983*. Edited by Helmuth Kiesel. 2nd exp. and rev. ed. Stuttgart: Klett-Cotta, 2012 [1999].

Schmitt, Carl, and Rudolf Smend. *"Auf der gefahrenvollen Straße des öffentlichen Rechts": Briefwechsel Carl Schmitt–Rudolf Smend, 1921–1961*. Edited by Reinhard Mehring. 2nd rev. ed. Berlin: Duncker & Humblot, 2012 [2010].

Schmitt, Carl, and Jacob Taubes. *Briefwechsel mit Materialien.* Edited by Herbert Kopp-Oberstebrink, Thorsten Palzhoff, and Martin Treml. Munich: Wilhelm Fink, 2012.

Schmitt, Carl, and Ernst Rudolf Huber. *Briefwechsel 1926–1981: Mit ergänzenden Materialien.* Edited by Ewald Grothe. Berlin: Duncker & Humblot, 2014.

## Editions of Works by Schmitt Available in English

Schmitt, Carl. *The Concept of the Political.* Translated by George Schwab. Chicago: University of Chicago Press, 1996 [1976].

Schmitt, Carl. *Political Theology: Four Chapters on the Concept of Sovereignty.* Translated by George Schwab. Chicago: University of Chicago Press, 2005 [1985].

Schmitt, Carl. *The Crisis of Parliamentary Democracy.* Translated by Ellen Kennedy. Cambridge, MA: The MIT Press, 1988 [1985].

Schmitt, Carl. "Interrogation of Carl Schmitt by Robert Kempner (I)–(III)." Translated by Joseph W. Bendersky. *Telos,* no. 72 (Summer 1987), pp. 97–105.

Schmitt, Carl. "The 'Fourth' (Second) Interrogation of Carl Schmitt." Edited with commentary and translated by Joseph W. Bendersky. *Telos,* no. 139 (Summer 2007), pp. 35–43.

Schmitt, Carl. *Roman Catholicism and Political Form.* Translated by G. L. Ulmen. Westport, CT: Greenwood Press, 1996.

Schmitt, Carl. *The Leviathan in the State Theory of Thomas Hobbes: Meaning and Failure of a Political Symbol.* Translated by George Schwab and Erna Hilfstein. Chicago: University of Chicago Press, 2008 [1996].

Schmitt, Carl. *The Nomos of the Earth in the International Law of the Jus Publicum Europaeum.* Translated by G. L. Ulmen. New York: Telos Press Publishing, 2003.

Schmitt, Carl. *Legality and Legitimacy*. Edited by Jeffrey Seitzer. Durham, NC: Duke Univ. Press, 2004.

Schmitt, Carl. *Theory of the Partisan: Intermediate Commentary on the Concept of the Political*. Translated by G. L. Ulmen. New York: Telos Press Publishing, 2007.

Schmitt, Carl. *Constitutional Theory*. Translated and edited by Jeffrey Seitzer. Durham, NC, and London: Duke Univ. Press, 2008.

Schmitt, Carl. *Political Theology II: The Myth of the Closure of any Political Theology*. Translated by Michael Hoelzl and Graham Ward. Cambridge: Polity Press, 2008.

Schmitt, Carl. *Hamlet or Hecuba: The Intrusion of the Time into the Play*. Translated by David Pan and Jennifer R. Rust. New York: Telos Press Publishing, 2009.

Schmitt, Carl. *Writings on War*. Translated and edited by Timothy Nunan. Cambridge: Polity Press, 2011.

Schmitt, Carl. *Dictatorship: From the Origin of the Modern Concept of Sovereignty to Proletarian Class Struggle*. Translated by Michael Hoelzl and Graham Ward. Cambridge: Polity Press, 2014.

Schmitt, Carl, and Hans Kelsen. *The Guardian of the Constitution: Hans Kelsen and Carl Schmitt on the Limits of Constitutional Law*. Edited and translated by Lars Vinx. Cambridge: Cambridge Univ. Press, 2015.

Schmitt, Carl. *Dialogues on Power and Space*. Translated by Samuel Garrett Zeitlin. Edited by Federico Finchelstein and Andreas Kalyvas. Cambridge: Polity Press, 2015.

## Secondary Literature on Schmitt in German

Benoist, Alain de. *Carl Schmitt: Bibliographie seiner Schriften und Korrespondenzen*. Berlin: Akademie Verlag, 2003.

Burkhardt, Kai, ed. *Carl Schmitt und die Öffentlichkeit: Briefwechsel mit Journalisten, Publizisten und Verlegern aus den Jahren 1923 bis 1983.* Berlin: Duncker & Humblot, 2013.

Groh, Ruth. *Carl Schmitts gnostischer Dualismus: Der boshafte Schöpfer dieser Welt hat es so eingerichtet (...).* Berlin-Münster: LIT Verlag, 2014.

Gross, Raphael. *Carl Schmitt und die Juden: Eine deutsche Rechtslehre.* Rev. and exp. ed. Frankfurt am Main: Suhrkamp Verlag, 2005 [2000].

Giesler, Gerd. "Nachwort." In Carl Schmitt, *Gespräch über die Macht und den Zugang zum Machthaber,* edited by Gerd Giesler, pp. 67–95. Stuttgart: Klett-Cotta, 2008.

Hertweck, Frank, and Dimitrios Kisoudis, eds. *"Solange das Imperium da ist": Carl Schmitt im Gespräch mit Klaus Figge und Dieter Groh 1971.* Berlin: Duncker & Humblot, 2010.

Laak, Dirk van. "Von Alfred T. Mahan zu Carl Schmitt: Das Verhältnis von Land- und Seemacht." In *Geopolitik: Grenzgänge im Zeitgeist,* edited by Irene Diekmann, Peter Krüger, and Julius H. Schoeps, vol. 1.1, pp. 257–82. Potsdam: Verlag für Berlin-Brandenburg, 2000.

Laak, Dirk van. *Gespräche in der Sicherheit des Schweigens: Carl Schmitt in der politischen Geistesgeschichte der frühen Bundesrepublik.* 2nd unrevised ed. Berlin: Akademie Verlag, 2002 [1993].

Mehring, Reinhard. *Carl Schmitt: Aufstieg und Fall.* Munich: C. H. Beck, 2009.

Mehring, Reinhard. *Carl Schmitt zur Einführung.* 4th completely rev. ed. Hamburg: Junius Verlag, 2011.

Meier, Heinrich. *Carl Schmitt, Leo Strauss und "Der Begriff des Politischen": Zu einem Dialog unter Abwesenden.* 3rd ed. Stuttgart/Weimar: Verlag J. B. Metzler, 2013 [1988].

Meier, Heinrich. *Die Lehre Carl Schmitts: Vier Kapitel zur Unterscheidung Politischer Theologie und Politischer Philosophie.* 3rd ed. Stuttgart/Weimar: Verlag J. B. Metzler, 2009 [1994].

Rüthers, Bernd. *Carl Schmitt im Dritten Reich.* 2nd exp. ed. Munich: C. H. Beck, 1990 [1989].

Schickel, Joachim. *Gespräche mit Carl Schmitt.* Berlin: Merve Verlag, 1993.

Sombart, Nicolaus. *Die deutschen Männer und ihre Feinde: Carl Schmitt—Ein deutsches Schicksal zwischen Männerbund und Matriachatsmythos.* Munich/Vienna: Carl Hanser Verlag, 1991.

Sombart, Nicolaus. *Jugend in Berlin, 1933–1943: Ein Bericht.* Munich/Vienna: Carl Hanser Verlag, 1984.

Taubes, Jacob. *Ad Carl Schmitt: Gegenstrebige Fügung.* Berlin: Merve Verlag, 1987.

Taubes, Jacob, ed. *Der Fürst dieser Welt: Carl Schmitt und die Folgen.* 2nd rev. ed. Vol. 1 of *Religionstheorie und Politische Theologie.* Munich/Paderborn/Vienna/Zurich: Wilhelm Fink Verlag/Verlag Ferdinand Schöningh, 1985 [1983].

Tommissen, Piet, ed. *Schmittiana V: Beiträge zum Leben und Werk Carl Schmitts.* Berlin: Duncker & Humblot, 1996.

Tielke, Martin. "Die Bibliothek Carl Schmitts." Carl Schmitt Gesellschaft, Stand 1.6.2015. http://www.carl-schmitt.de/download/biblio-cs.pdf (accessed on June 26, 2015).

Tielke, Martin. *Der stille Bürgerkrieg: Ernst Jünger und Carl Schmitt im Dritten Reich.* Berlin: Landt Verlag, 2007.

## Secondary Literature on Schmitt in English

Balakrishnan, Gopal. *The Enemy: An Intellectual Portrait of Carl Schmitt.* London and New York: Verso, 2000.

Bendersky, Joseph W. *Carl Schmitt: Theorist for the Reich.* Princeton, NJ: Princeton Univ. Press, 1983.

Connery, Christopher L. "Ideologies of Land and Sea: Alfred Thayer Mahan, Carl Schmitt, and the Shaping of Global Myth Elements." *boundary 2*, vol. 28, no. 2 (Summer 2001), pp. 173–201.

Derman, Joshua. "Carl Schmitt on Land and Sea." *History of European Ideas*, vol. 37, no. 2 (2011), pp. 181–89.

Dyzenhaus, David. *Legality and Legitimacy: Carl Schmitt, Hans Kelsen, and Hermann Heller in Weimar*. Oxford: Oxford Univ. Press, 1997.

Dyzenhaus, David, ed. *Law as Politics: Carl Schmitt's Critique of Liberalism*. Durham, NC: Duke Univ. Press, 1998.

Elden, Stuart. "Reading Schmitt Geopolitically: Nomos, Territory and *Großraum*." In *Spatiality, Sovereignty and Carl Schmitt: Geographies of the Nomos*, edited by Stephen Legg, pp. 91–105. London: Routledge, 2011.

Gordon, Peter E., and John P. McCormick, eds. *Weimar Thought: A Contested Legacy*. Princeton, NJ: Princeton Univ. Press, 2013.

Gross, Rafael. *Carl Schmitt and the Jews: The "Jewish Question," the Holocaust, and German Legal Theory*. Translated by Joel Golb. Madison: Univ. of Wisconsin Press, 2007.

Hammill, Graham, and Julia Reinhard Lupton, eds. *Political Theology and Early Modernity*. Chicago: Univ. of Chicago Press, 2012.

Hoelzl, Michael, and Graham Ward. "Editor's Introduction." In Carl Schmitt, *Political Theology II: The Myth of the Closure of any Political Theology*, translated by Michael Hoelzl and Graham Ward, pp. 1–29. Cambridge: Polity Press, 2008.

Hoelzl, Michael, and Graham Ward. "Introduction." In Carl Schmitt, *Dictatorship: From the Origin of the Modern Concept of Sovereignty to Proletarian Class Struggle*, translated by Michael Hoelzl and Graham Ward, pp. x–xxix. Cambridge: Polity Press, 2014.

Hooker, William. *Carl Schmitt's International Thought: Order and Orientation.* Cambridge: Cambridge Univ. Press, 2009.

Howse, Robert. "From Legitimacy to Dictatorship—and Back Again: Leo Strauss's Critique of the Anti-Liberalism of Carl Schmitt." In *Law as Politics: Carl Schmitt's Critique of Liberalism,* edited by David Dyzenhaus, pp. 56–91. Durham, NC: Duke Univ. Press, 1998.

Hussain, Nasser. "Air Power." In *Spatiality, Sovereignty and Carl Schmitt: Geographies of the Nomos,* edited by Stephen Legg, pp. 244–50. London: Routledge, 2011.

Kahn, Victoria. *The Future of Illusion: Political Theology and Early Modern Texts.* Chicago: Univ. of Chicago Press, 2014.

Kahn, Victoria. "Hamlet or Hecuba: Carl Schmitt's Decision." *Representations,* vol. 83, no. 1 (Summer 2003), pp. 67–96.

Kennedy, Ellen. "Carl Schmitt and the Frankfurt School." *Telos,* no. 71 (Spring 1987), pp. 37–66.

Kennedy, Ellen. "*Hostis* Not *Inimicus*: Toward a Theory of the Public in the Work of Carl Schmitt." In *Law as Politics: Carl Schmitt's Critique of Liberalism,* edited by David Dyzenhaus, pp. 92–108. Durham, NC: Duke Univ. Press, 1998.

Kennedy, Ellen. *Constitutional Failure: Carl Schmitt in Weimar.* Durham, NC: Duke Univ. Press, 2004.

Kennedy, Ellen. "Introduction: Carl Schmitt's *Parlamentarismus* in Its Historical Context." In Carl Schmitt, *The Crisis of Parliamentary Democracy,* translated by Ellen Kennedy, pp. xiii–l. Cambridge, MA: The MIT Press, 1988 [1985].

McCormick, John P. *Carl Schmitt's Critique of Liberalism: Against Politics as Technology.* Cambridge: Cambridge Univ. Press, 1997.

McCormick, John P. "The Dilemmas of Dictatorship: Carl Schmitt and Constitutional Emergency Powers." In *Law as Politics: Carl Schmitt's Critique of Liberalism,* edited by

David Dyzenhaus, pp. 217–51. Durham, NC: Duke Univ. Press, 1998.

McCormick, John P. "Legal Theory and the Weimar Crisis of Law and Social Change." In *Weimar Thought: A Contested Legacy*, edited by Peter E. Gordon and John P. McCormick, pp. 55–71. Princeton, NJ: Princeton Univ. Press, 2013.

Mendieta, Eduardo. "*Land and Sea*." In *Spatiality, Sovereignty and Carl Schmitt: Geographies of the Nomos*, edited by Stephen Legg, pp. 260–67. London: Routledge, 2011.

Minkov, Svetozar, and Piotr Nowak, eds. *Man and His Enemies: Essays on Carl Schmitt*. Bialystock: Bialystock Univ. Press, 2008.

Mouffe, Chantal. "Carl Schmitt and the Paradox of Liberal Democracy." In *Law as Politics: Carl Schmitt's Critique of Liberalism*, edited by David Dyzenhaus, pp. 159–75. Durham, NC: Duke Univ. Press, 1998.

Mouffe, Chantal, ed. *The Challenge of Carl Schmitt*. London: Verso, 1999.

Müller, Jan-Werner. *A Dangerous Mind: Carl Schmitt in Post-War European Thought*. New Haven, CT, and London: Yale Univ. Press, 2003.

Newman, Jane O. *Benjamin's Library: Modernity, Nation, and the Baroque*. Ithaca, NY: Cornell Univ. Press, 2011.

Nunan, Timothy. "Notes on the Text." In Carl Schmitt, *Writings on War*, edited by Timothy Nunan, pp. 75–76. Cambridge: Polity Press, 2011.

Nunan, Timothy. "Translator's Introduction." In Carl Schmitt, *Writings on War*, edited by Timothy Nunan, pp. 1–26. Cambridge: Polity Press, 2011.

Pan, David. "Afterword: Historical Event and Mythic Meaning in Carl Schmitt's *Hamlet or Hecuba*." In Carl Schmitt, *Hamlet or Hecuba: The Intrusion of the Time into the Play*, translated by David Pan and Jennifer R. Rust, pp. 69–119. New York: Telos Press Publishing, 2009.

Pan, David, and Russell A. Berman. "Introduction." *Telos*, no. 142 (Spring 2008), pp. 3–6.

Ragazzoni, David. "Carl Schmitt and Global (Dis)Order at the Twilight of the *Jus Publicum Europaeum*." *Journal of Intellectual History and Political Thought*, no. 2 (2013), pp. 170–91.

Rust, Jennifer R., and Julia Reinhard Lupton. "Introduction: Schmitt and Shakespeare." In Carl Schmitt, *Hamlet or Hecuba: The Intrusion of the Time into the Play*, translated by David Pan and Jennifer R. Rust, pp. xv–li. New York: Telos Press Publishing, 2009.

Scheuerman, William E. *Carl Schmitt: The End of Law*. Lanham, MD: Rowman & Littlefield, 1999.

Scheuerman, William E. "International Law as Historical Myth." *Constellations*, vol. 11, no. 4 (2004), pp. 537–50.

Schwab, George. *The Challenge of the Exception: An Introduction to the Political Ideas of Carl Schmitt Between 1921 and 1936*. Westport, CT: Greenwood Press, 1989 [1970].

Schwab, George. "Introduction." In Carl Schmitt, *Political Theology: Four Chapters on the Concept of Sovereignty*, translated by George Schwab, pp. xxxvii–lii. Chicago: Univ. of Chicago Press, 2005 [1985].

Schwab, George. "Introduction." In Carl Schmitt, *The Leviathan in the State Theory of Thomas Hobbes: Meaning and Failure of a Political Symbol*, translated by George Schwab and Erna Hilfstein, pp. xxxi–liii. Chicago: Univ. of Chicago Press, 2008.

Seitzer, Jeffrey. *Comparative History and Legal Theory: Carl Schmitt in the First German Democracy*. Westport, CT: Greenwood Press, 2001.

Seitzer, Jeffrey, and Christopher Thornhill. "An Introduction to Carl Schmitt's *Constitutional Theory*: Issues and Context." In

Carl Schmitt, *Constitutional Theory*, edited by Jeffrey Seitzer, pp. 1–50. Durham, NC, and London: Duke Univ. Press, 2008.

Stirk, Peter. "Carl Schmitt's *Völkerrechtliche Großraumordnung*." *History of Political Thought*, vol. 20, no. 2 (Summer 1999), pp. 357–74.

Strong, Tracy B. "Foreword: Dimensions of the New Debate Around Carl Schmitt." In Carl Schmitt, *The Concept of the Political*, translated by George Schwab, pp. ix–xxvii. Chicago: University of Chicago Press, 1996.

Strong, Tracy B. "Foreword: Carl Schmitt and Thomas Hobbes: Myth and Politics." In Carl Schmitt, *The Leviathan in the State Theory of Thomas Hobbes: Meaning and Failure of a Political Symbol*, translated by George Schwab and Erna Hilfstein, pp. vii–xxviii. Chicago: Univ. of Chicago Press, 2008.

Strong, Tracy B. "Foreword: The Sovereign and the Exception: Carl Schmitt, Politics, Theology, and Leadership." In Carl Schmitt, *Political Theology: Four Chapters on the Concept of Sovereignty*, translated by George Schwab, pp. vii–xxxiii. Chicago: Univ. of Chicago Press, 2005.

Vatter, Miguel. "The Idea of Public Reason and Reason of State: Schmitt and Rawls on the Political." *Political Theory*, vol. 36, no. 2 (April 2008), pp. 239–71.

Vatter, Miguel. "Schmitt and Strauss as Readers of Hobbes and Spinoza: On the Relation between Political Theology and Liberalism." *The New Centennial Review*, vol. 4, no. 3 (Winter 2004), pp. 161–214.

Vinx, Lars. "Introduction." In *The Guardian of the Constitution: Hans Kelsen and Carl Schmitt on the Limits of Constitutional Law*, edited and translated by Lars Vinx, pp. 1–21. Cambridge: Cambridge Univ. Press, 2015.

Weinreich, Max. *Hitler's Professors: The Part of Scholarship in Germany's Crimes Against the Jewish People*. New Haven, CT, and London: Yale Univ. Press, 1999 [1946].

## Other Works Consulted

Armitage, David. "The Elephant and the Whale: Empires of Land and Sea." *Journal of Maritime History*, vol. 9, no. 1 (2007), pp. 23–36.

Bendersky, Joseph. *A Concise History of Nazi Germany*. 4th ed. Lanham, MD: Rowman & Littlefield, 2014.

Davidowicz, Lucy S. *The War Against the Jews, 1933–1945*. New York: Bantam Books, 1979 [1975].

Depeyre, Michel. "Clerk, John, of Eldin (1728–1812)." In *Oxford Dictionary of National Biography*. Oxford: Oxford Univ. Press, 2004. http://www.oxforddnb.com/view/article/5618 (accessed June 13, 2014).

Diekmann, Irene, Peter Krüger, and Julius H. Schoeps, eds. *Geopolitik: Grenzgänge im Zeitgeist*. Potsdam: Verlag für Berlin-Brandenburg, 2000.

Edelstein, Dan. "*Hostis Humani Generis*: Devils, Natural Right, and Terror in the French Revolution." *Telos*, no. 141 (Winter 2007), pp. 57–81.

Evans, Richard J. *The Third Reich at War: How the Nazis Led Germany from Conquest to Disaster*. London: Penguin Books, 2009 [2008].

Freund, Julien. "Introduction." In Carl Schmitt, *Terre et mer: Un point de vue sur l'histoire mondiale*, translated by Jean-Louis Pesteil, pp. 9–16. Paris: Éditions du Labyrinthe, 1985.

Freund, Julien. "Postface: La thalassopolitique." In Carl Schmitt, *Terre et mer: Un point de vue sur l'histoire mondiale*, translated by Jean-Louis Pesteil, pp. 91–121. Paris: Éditions du Labyrinthe, 1985.

Gelderen, Martin van. *The Political Thought of the Dutch Revolt, 1555-1590.* Cambridge: Cambridge Univ. Press, 1992.

Hauner, Milan. *Hitler: A Chronology of His Life and Time.* Basingstoke: Palgrave Macmillan, 2005.

Heine, Heinrich. *Sämtliche Gedichte: Kommentierte Ausgabe.* Edited by Bernd Kortländer. Stuttgart: Philipp Reclam jun., 2009 [1990]

Heller-Roazen, Daniel. *The Enemy of All: Piracy and the Law of Nations.* New York: Zone Books, 2009.

Herf, Jeffrey. *The Jewish Enemy: Nazi Propaganda During World War II and the Holocaust.* Cambridge, MA: Belknap Press of Harvard Univ. Press, 2006.

Herf, Jeffrey. *Nazi Propaganda for the Arab World.* New Haven, CT: Yale Univ. Press, 2010 [2009].

Inwood, Brad, ed. *The Poem of Empedocles: A Text and Translation with an Introduction.* Rev. ed. Toronto: Univ. of Toronto Press, 2001 [1992].

Jünger, Ernst. *Strahlungen I.* In *Tagebücher II*, vol. 2 of *Tagebücher*, from *Sämtliche Werke in Achtzehn Bänden.* Stuttgart: Klett-Cotta, 1979 [1949].

Kershaw, Ian. *Hitler 1936–1945: Nemesis.* London: Penguin Books, 2001 [2000].

Koskenniemi, Martti. *The Gentle Civilizer of Nations: The Rise and Fall of International Law 1870–1960.* Cambridge: Cambridge Univ. Press, 2001.

Mansfeld, Jaap, and Oliver Primavesi, eds. *Die Vorsokratiker: Griechisch/Deutsch.* Reissue. Stuttgart: Philipp Reclam jun. GmbH, 2012 [2011].

Mazower, Mark. *Hitler's Empire: Nazi Rule in Occupied Europe.* London: Penguin Books, 2009 [2008].

Motadel, David. *Islam and Nazi Germany's War.* Cambridge, MA: Belknap Press of Harvard Univ. Press, 2014.

Tielke, Martin. "Die Bibliothek Carl Schmitts (Monographien)." Carl-Schmitt-Gesellschaft. http://www.carl-schmitt.de/download/biblio-cs.pdf (accessed April 15, 2015).

Volpi, Franco. "Il potere degli elementi." In Carl Schmitt, *Terra e Mare: Una riflessione sulla storia del mondo*, translated by Giovanni Gurisatti, 5th ed., pp. 113–49. Milan: Adelphi Edizioni, 2011 [2002].

Zarka, Yves Charles. *Un détail nazi dans la pensée de Carl Schmitt*. Paris: Presses Universitaires de France, 2005.

Zaslavsky, Victor. *Class Cleansing: The Massacre at Katyn*. Translated by Kizer Walker. New York: Telos Press Publishing, 2008.

# Also from Telos Press Publishing

*The* Nomos *of the Earth
in the International Law of the* Jus Publicum Europaeum
Carl Schmitt

*Theory of the Partisan*
Carl Schmitt

*Hamlet or Hecuba:
The Intrusion of the Time into the Play*
Carl Schmitt

*Eumeswil*
Ernst Jünger

*The Forest Passage*
Ernst Jünger

*On Pain*
Ernst Jünger

*The Adventurous Heart: Figures and Capriccios*
Ernst Jünger

*Germany and Iran
From the Aryan Axis to the Nuclear Threshold*
Matthias Küntzel

*The New Class Conflict*
Joel Kotkin

*Confronting the Crisis: Writings of Paul Piccone*
Paul Piccone

*A Journal of No Illusions:
Telos, Paul Piccone, and the Americanization of Critical Theory*
Timothy W. Luke and Ben Agger, eds.

# Praise for Carl Schmitt's *Land and Sea*

"Schmitt's 'Dialogue of Land and Sea' is an extraordinary text: erudite, bizarre, philosophic, and theatrical. Who but Schmitt would name a character 'MacFuture'? Who else could revive the dialogue form to interrogate modernity? Who else could conduct a dialogue with Heidegger between the lines of a mid-twentieth-century radio play? Zeitlin has given us a great gift in translating this curious, complex, and very entertaining dialogue."

—**Anne Norton**, Professor of Political Science,
University of Pennsylvania.

"Samuel Zeitlin has given us a careful and very readable English translation of one Schmitt's key texts on the philosophy of history and the foundations of international law. *Land and Sea* illuminates the theoretical background of Schmitt's theory of the '*nomos* of the Earth,' and it is supplemented by a valuable introduction and helpful editorial notes. The volume is required reading for all scholars seriously interested in Schmitt."

—**Lars Vinx**, Assistant Professor of Philosophy at Bilkent University, author of the *Stanford Encyclopedia of Philosophy* entry on Schmitt, and editor and translator of *The Guardian of the Constitution: Hans Kelsen and Carl Schmitt on the Limits of Constitutional Law* (Cambridge University Press, 2015)

"With its fable-like quality, philosophical tone, and deep historical orientation, *Land and Sea* is one of Schmitt's most powerful and evocative works. A profound meditation on the forces shaping twentieth-century history, it challenges us to think anew about the possibilities (and risks) of our global future. Yet, as Zeitlin's meticulous introduction demonstrates so clearly, the origins of Schmitt's thinking on these themes must be traced to the specific political and military ambitions of the Third Reich. This tension between Schmitt's grand philosophical history (fluidly translated here) and the often brutal concreteness of its compositional context makes Land and Sea an even more fascinating—if troubling—work."

—**David Bates**, Professor and Chair, Department of Rhetoric,
University of California, Berkeley